HIKES & WALKS
on
MT HOOD

Government Camp & Timberline Lodge Area

Sonia Buist & Emily Keller

LOLITS Press
Portland, Oregon

Printed in Portland, Oregon

Library of Congress Catalog Number 94-72941
International Standard Book Number 09643836-0-8

Writer and Editor   Sonia Buist
Illustrations, Maps and Cover   Emily Keller
Designer and Project Manager   Judith Rose
Layout   Neil McKamey
Type and Printing   Network Graphics
Bindery   Lincoln & Allen

To order copies of *Hikes and Walks on Mt. Hood*,
see the coupon enclosed with this book, or write:

LOLITS Press
8510 SW White Pine Lane
Portland, OR 97225

10 9 8 7 6 5 4 3 2 1

12/25/1996

TABLE OF CONTENTS

ACKNOWLEDGEMENTS

We would like to acknowledge the help and support we got for this project from our husbands, Neil and Paul, our families and friends. We would also like to acknowledge the contibutions of Emily Park who hiked many of the trails with us, Martie Sucec and Linda Zucker who helped with editing, Cindy Brandt who spent many hours on formatting, and Bruce Haynes and Terry Sroufe of the US Forest Service who provided invaluable advice.

We would like to acknowledge the many friends who helped by testing out our instructions and maps. We are happy to say that they all came back safely although one did hike the extra mile! The roll of honor includes:

Cecille & Gary Beyl

Rose Bond

Wendy Bjornson

Dady Blake

Diana, Catriona
& Alison Buist

Steve Bussler

Bob & Carol Carson

Jack Fellman & Chloe

David Gonzales

Carla Green

Pat Harwood

Susan Katz

Nancy Kennaway

Kate LaGrande

Greg & Kathy Link

Jan, Bill & Cameron Madill

Phillipe, Julianne
& Andrew Masser

Jim Morris

Mary Ellen Mogren

Deanna & Wilfried
Mueller Crispin

George Nash

Casey O'Hearn

Molly Osborne

Lynn Oveson

Betty Parker

Julianne Penco

Patricia Reilly

Adam, Eric, Jean & Bill
Vollmer

Jennifer Sagaser

Mary Schick

Kate Sutherland

Jane & David Turville

Dirk Wahlers

Adele Wilson

Margin Wall

Tina Webster

Carolyn Wood

Linda Zucker

INTRODUCTION

Oregon has a well-deserved reputation for its natural beauty. It is less renowned for its hiking trails although few countries, much less states, match them for range and variety. We are particularly fortunate in having two spectacular areas for hiking within 60 miles of Portland—the Columbia Gorge and the Mt Hood areas.

This book focuses on the Government Camp and Timberline Lodge areas on Mt Hood, both close enough to Portland for half-day or day hikes. Both areas offer magnificent mountain scenery, beautiful forests—some with majestic old growth trees—streams, rivers, wetlands, abundant flowers, birds and glimpses of wildlife.

We hope that this book will serve to introduce you to new walking and hiking trails and areas. We have tried to include hikes that cover a range of difficulty and challenge, from a short walk suitable for those with limited mobility, to trails with appreciable elevation gain and difficult terrain. We encourage you to try some new hikes and venture away from the heavily-used trails.

We wanted to make this a book that tucks comfortably into a pocket. This imposed constraints on the amount of text we could include and on the size of maps. Our overriding aim was to be precise and accurate. We hope we have struck a balance that works for most people.

HIKING SAFETY

It is a good idea to take extra clothing, food and water, however briefly you expect to be out on the trail. Even better is to get in the habit of keeping a small hiking kit packed with the 10 hiking essentials, and taking it with you whenever you go out on the trails. The Mazama Mountaineering Club recommends the following 10 Essentials:

1. Whistle
2. Map
3. Compass
4. Flashlight
5. Extra food and clothing
6. Knife
7. First Aid Kit
8. Matches in waterproof container
9. Firestarter or candle
10. Sunglasses & sun/wind-burn cream

Item #2 on this list is a map. We recommend the USGS maps, available at many outdoor stores and the US Forest Service, and list the appropriate map for each hike. We also recommend the Mt Hood Wilderness Map, available at the same locations. It covers the Government Camp and Timberline Lodge areas and shows most of the trails included in this book.

IT IS NOT A GOOD IDEA TO HIKE ALONE. If you do, you might want to consider taking a cellular phone—and be sure to tell someone where you are going!

HOW TO USE THIS BOOK

We have tried to provide guidance as to the relative difficulty of the trails, and the noteworthy features of each hike. To rank the trails by difficulty, we have taken into account the length, elevation gain, smoothness of the trail, and the altitude at which you are hiking. These criteria are reflected in our category designations: Easy; Moderate; Moderately strenuous; and Strenuous.

We have also given an approximate time for the hike, recognising that people vary in their hiking pace and in the time they like to spend enjoying the scenery, identifying the flowers, taking photographs, and just lingering.

Since this book focusses on the Government Camp and Timberline Lodge areas of Mt Hood, we have referenced all of the directions to a central point—the Summit Rest Area at the far (east) end of the Government Camp business loop. This is a convenient meeting place with ample parking, public toilets, a gas station and cafe.

It takes about 1 1/2 hours to drive the 57 miles to Government Camp from Portland. To reach Government Camp, take I-84 east from Portland to the Wood Village exit, about 15 miles from the city center. Turn right, continue on this road for almost 3 miles through Wood Village and part of Gresham, and turn left onto Burnside. In about 1 mile, Burnside becomes Hwy 26. Continue straight (east) on Hwy 26 for 38 miles to Government Camp.

LEGEND

Indicates North	N
Indicates direction (**not actual position**) of Mt. Hood	
Directions begin from here	
Summit Ski Rest Area	
Building	
Campground	
Ski lift	
Trail	••••••
Main road	▬▬▬▬▬
Paved or good gravel	▬▬
Service or rough woods road	= = = =
Power lines	—·—·—·—

IN AND AROUND GOVERNMENT CAMP

We describe two walks in and around Government
Camp village. One is a delightful new trail that loops
through the forest north of the village and connects
Glacier View Snopark by Enid Lake—to the west of
Government Camp—and Summit Ski Area at the east
end of the village. You can access this trail from several
places in Government Camp. The other trail connects
the Summit Rest Area and Ski Area with Ski Bowl East
and West. You can combine the two trails to make a
4-mile loop. There is a cafe at Summit and at Ski Bowl,
and plenty of parking at both.

Near Government Camp

CROSSTOWN TRAIL

Easy

2 miles one way, 1–1½ hours; 4 miles roundtrip, 2–3 hours

Maps: USGS, Government Camp & Mt Hood South Quadrangle

Description: A delightful new multi-purpose trail (#755) that loops to the north of Government Camp and links the Glacier View Snopark west of the village and the Summit Ski Area at the east end of the village. In winter, the trail will be used for cross-country skiing, and in summer for hiking and mountain biking. This trail can be hiked one way, with a car shuttle, or as a loop. You can also access it from several places in Government Camp.

Car shuttle: Leave one car at the Glacier View Snopark and the other at the Summit Rest Area.

Access: 1) *To hike from west to east,* drive 1½ miles west on Hwy 26 from the Summit Rest Area at the far (east) end of the Government Camp business loop and turn right onto Road #552 between mileposts 52 and 53—almost opposite the west entrance to Ski Bowl West. Glacier View Snopark, about 200 yards from the highway, offers ample parking. Several trails meet here, so take care to find the right one. At press time, the Crosstown Trail was not yet signed. Until it is, follow the signs for the Enid Lake Loop Ski trail easily seen on the right from the parking area. The trail heads north towards Enid Lake—little more than a muddy puddle in summer—and just before it reaches the lake, the new, broad trail turns to the right and loops round to the east and north of Enid Lake before curving northeast towards Mt Hood above Government Camp. At the first fork, turn right to go to the Thunderbird Condos at the west end of the village, or left to continue on to the Summit Ski Area. The trail crosses a service road, then continues on over several streams crossed by sturdy new bridges. The trail crosses one more service road before reaching Summit Ski Area and the Summit Rest Area. The hike can be shortened by turning right (south) onto Glade Trail and down into Government Camp.

2) *To hike from east to west,* park at the Summit Rest area and walk up the service road on the left side of the main ski run, behind the Day Lodge, to the point where the power lines cross, just above the last house. Turn left (west) and almost immediately find the beginning of the new trail on your right. The trail heads towards the trees and continues into the forest, crosses a service road, several bridges, Glade Trail, and another service road on its way to Enid Lake and the Glacier View Snopark. You can shorten the hike by turning down any of the roads to the village.

Features: This is a most welcome addition to the walks and hikes in the Government Camp area, with a section of exquisite forest of second growth trees mixed with some majestic old growth. Moss carpets the forest floor on the western segment of the hike, and several pretty streams cross the trail on the eastern part. Mt Hood keeps popping up through the trees. Lots of flowers and beargrass bloom in the spring and summer, with huckleberries available near Enid Lake in August and mushrooms in fall.

Optional addition: This hike can be made into an interesting loop by combining it with the Summit Trail (see page 14).

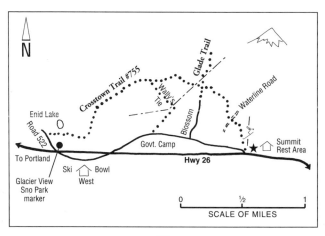

SUMMIT TRAIL TO SKI BOWL
Easy (almost flat service roads)
1¾ miles each way, 1–1½ hours each way
Maps: USGS, Government Camp and Mt Hood
**   South Quadrangles**

Description: A gentle walk along a mostly flat forest service road through a section of majestic old growth trees and across Ski Bowl East ski area.

Access: From the Summit Rest Area at the far (east) end of Government Camp, cross Hwy 26 and follow the paved service road that takes off on the south side of the highway at milepost 54. The paving stops at the substation and the road continues as a forest road. Follow this for almost a mile to Ski Bowl East Day Lodge, and pick up another service road heading in the same direction, just to the right of and below the Day Lodge. This road passes a chairlift and ropetow, meets up with the bottom end of Multorpor Chairlift, and curves up and to the right and heads for Ski Bowl West through the trees. When the road emerges from the trees, it divides—keep straight on to the Day Lodge; the right curves back and meets Hwy 26 at the east end of the Ski Bowl loop.

Features: This is an easy walk with beautiful views of Mt Hood, magnificent old growth trees, and flowers along the way. A car shuttle makes this hike only 1¾ miles. The Alpine Slide at Ski Bowl, or the cafes at both Ski Bowl and Summit may be added enticements.

Douglas Fir Cone

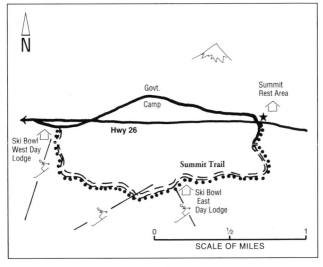

EAST AND SOUTH OF GOVERNMENT CAMP

The area east and south of Government Camp offers a variety of one-way trails and loops. Most, but not all, entail some elevation gain or loss, but they are not difficult or steep. Most of the hikes and walks are on well-maintained trails or forest roads, some are on winter ski trails, and most are through second growth mixed forest of Douglas fir, hemlock and cedar. Many of these trails and roads are thought of as winter nordic ski trails, and not as summer hiking trails. This is a pity because they are beautiful summer trails and have much of interest to offer the hiker. All are perfect for a half day hike or for a very leisurely day hike with frequent stops to identify flowers, take photos, or dabble in the streams.

There are opportunities to put together combinations of trails and loops to meet every interest, and level of fitness or energy. You are only limited by your stamina and the time available. All of the trails in this section can be accessed from Government Camp, and instructions for finding the trail use the Summit Rest Area at the far (east) end of the Government Camp business loop as a reference. On trails that allow both hikers and mountain bikes, hikers should give way to bikes.

Summit Meadow

SUMMIT MEADOW AND PIONEER BABY'S GRAVE

Easy
3 miles roundtrip, 1½–2 hours
Map: USGS, Mt Hood South Quadrangle

Description: A delightful, easy hike, part on the old Barlow wagon road, part on a paved forest road. The goal of the hike is the beautiful Summit Meadow, where the pioneers and their livestock rested before pushing on to the difficult stretch to the west. The portion of the hike on the paved Still Creek road provides access to Still Creek Campground and Trillium Lake, so watch out for cars.

Access: Park at the Summit Rest Area at the far (east) end of the Government Camp business loop, cross Hwy 26, and find an unpaved road leading to Forest Service cabins, just *after* milepost 54. The trail starts behind the cabins and is marked by a ski trail sign to Barlow Trail and Summit Meadow, and then by an Oregon Trail post since this is part of the old Barlow wagon trail. The trail meets a clearcut after about 100 yeards, then re-enters the forest. Ignore the trail to the left in the clearcut. Soon after the trail re-enters the forest, it is joined on the right by a tie trail to the Summit trail, and continues gently downhill for about ½ mile until it crosses Still Creek and joins the paved road through Still Creek Campground. Turn right on to the paved road and follow it through the campground and on to Summit Meadow. The paving ends just after the campground and the road passes several private cabins. At the beginning of the meadow, there is a junction. To find the Pioneer Baby's grave, keep going straight: the grave is a few yards further, on the right, and is fenced. Return the same way.

Features: This is a gentle hike through beautiful forest, with the added historical interest that it follows a portion of the old Barlow wagon road. Summit Meadow provides a truly spectacular view of Mt Hood and a magificent display of wildflowers. The Pioneer Baby's grave is where the infant son of William Barclay was buried after his mother had died on the trail and the baby was fatally injured in an accident. Perry Vickers built the first log cabin here in 1866, and Summit Meadow became another tollgate.

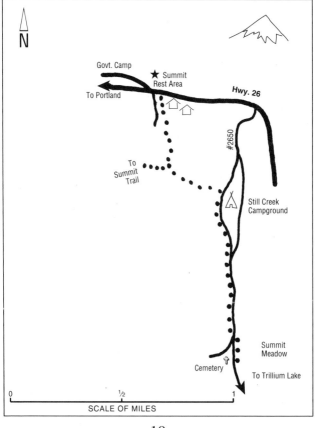

MULTORPOR MOUNTAIN LOOP

Moderate (mostly flat or gentle grades; short steep uphill section)

3¾-mile loop, 2–3 hours

Maps: USGS, Government Camp and Mt Hood South

Description: A new trail around Multorpor Mountain, made for mountain bikers. The trail weaves through fairly dense forest in some sections, so keep a sharp eye and ear out for the bikers–and give way to them. Mostly gentle grades, though there is a steep pitch lasting about ¼ mile towards the end of the hike. This is a delightful addition to the hikes in this area.

Access: Park at the Summit Rest Area at the far (east) end of the Government Camp business loop, cross Hwy 26 and follow the service road beside milepost 54. Pass the power substation and follow the road for ¼ mile to where it bends to the right. About 50 yards further, turn left onto a service road beside a power line and follow the road and power line up a short hill, then down a hill and to the right (leaving the power line) to a clearing where the road becomes indistinct. The new bike trail takes off to the right at the start of the clearing. From here, the trail meanders through a magical forest, dense in some places and more open in others. Keep following the new bike trail until it meets a rock road, and then follow this to the right until the rock surface ends and the road bends to the right. The bike trail continues straight at this point, beside a stream, and soon starts to climb quite steeply for about ¼ mile. At the top of the hill, the trail emerges to join one of the ski runs at Ski Bowl East. Follow any of the several service roads to the right to the Ski Bowl East Day Lodge. The service road (Summit Trail) that leads back to the Summit Rest Area takes off and heads east just past and above the Day Lodge.

Features: This beautiful hike has much to offer: lots of flowers; some magnificent old growth trees and stumps; a forest that seems to change in character at every turn. Some relatively dense patches alternate with more open stretches that offer views of meadows and the back of the Upper Bowl of Ski Bowl; and, towards the end of the hike, a stream with exquisite small pools and basins and moss-covered rocks. In the spring, as soon as the snow melts, there is a profusion of flowers: anemones, vetch, yellow violets, trillium, orchids, Indian paintbrush, vanilla leaf, marsh marigolds, skunk cabbage and wild stawberries. In June, the rhododendrons are in full bloom and later there are lupine and banks of twin flowers. In August, the huckleberries are ready to pick. Remember to watch and listen for bicyclists—this is their trail!

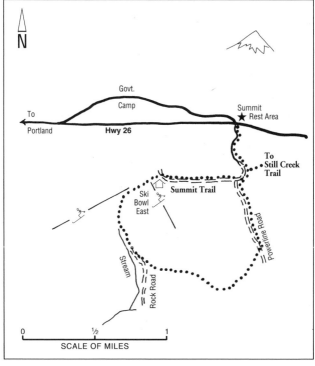

MULTORPOR MOUNTAIN VIEWPOINT
Moderate (short, but steep)
2½ miles roundtrip, 1½–2 hours
Map: USGS, Mt Hood South Quadrangle

Description: A steep but short climb on an unmarked and unmaintained trail to the top of Multorpor Mountain. Fantastic views in every direction. The steepness and unevenness of the trial makes the descent a little tricky.

Access: Park at the Summit Rest Area at the far (east) end of the Government Camp business loop, cross Hwy 26 and follow the service road beside milepost 54. Pass the power substation and follow the road for ¼ mile to where it bends to the right. About 50 yards further, turn left onto a service road beside a power line. Follow this up a short hill and just after the crest of the hill, as the road is going downhill, find an unmarked, but clearly visible trail on the right heading straight up Multorpor Mountain. The trail climbs steadily and quite steeply to the viewpoint at the top. Return the same way.

Vine Maple

Features: This short, steep hike offers a spectacular, bird's eye view of the area: north to Government Camp and Mt Hood, south to Summit Meadows, Trillium Lake, and Still Creek, and west to Tom, Dick and Harry Mountain and Zigzag Valley. The flute-like song of the hermit thrush provides a musical accompaniment. Bunchberries, several different penstemon, paintbrush, cat's ear lily, vanilla leaf, beargrass, anemones, lupine, pyrola, and clintonia can be seen beside the trail.

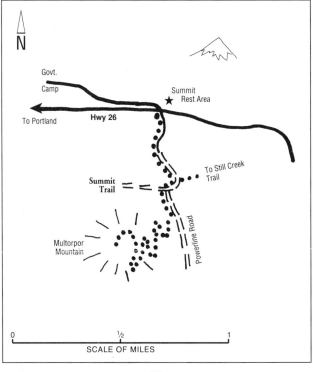

WEST YELLOWJACKET LOOP
Moderate (700 ft elevation gain, trail indistinct in places)
5 mile loop, 3–4 hours
Map: USGS, Mt Hood South Quadrangle

Description: A delightful loop that is better known as a cross-country ski trail (#674). For some parts of the trail, the path is not obvious, but it is always easy to follow the trail by following the blue diamond-shaped ski trail markers high on the trees. This hike provides plenty of variety, some lovely views of Mt Hood, beautiful forest, and pockets of wetland. A very accessible hike offering a fine reward for following the less trodden path. This hike requires a sense of adventure.

Access: Park at the Summit Rest Area at the far (east) end of the Government Camp business loop and follow the service road up the left side of Summit Ski Area, behind the Day Lodge, to the top of the chairlift. Continue on the forest road to the left of the chairlift terminus. This is the end of Alpine ski trail from Timberline Lodge. Follow Alpine Trail for about ⅓ mile until you can see paved West Leg Road (the old road to Timberline Lodge) on the right, close to the trail. Turn left onto West Leg Road and follow it for about ½ mile to a left-hand bend where an unpaved road takes off to the right, signed as the Tie Trail to Snowbunny Lodge. Follow the Tie Trail down a gentle grade until it meets and crosses Timberline Road. After crossing, continue down the Tie Trail for about 200 yards to a fork. Take the right fork (Rd #149) and just before the road bends to the left, look high up on the bank and see a sign for Yellowjacket Ski Trail. Climb the bank and look for blue diamond-shaped ski trail markers on the trees. Follow these markers, always keeping the next set of markers in sight. This is especially important in the area that has been logged recently. At one point, the trail meets a logging road. Turn right and follow the road for 100 yards, watching for the blue markers, and find the continuation of Yellowjacket Trail on the left of the road. In another section the trail crosses a clearcut. The trail twists and turns and continues gradually downhill through the forest and comes out just above the junction of Timberline Road and Hwy 26. Watch for a black arrow in the blue ski trail markers in a few places where the trail takes a turn, including just before the trail ends at its junction with Timberline Road.

Features: This loop has a lot to offer: spectacular views of Mt Hood; a sporting combination of easy forest roads and lightly-used crosscountry ski trails through open forest; new growth forest juxtaposed with some majestic old growth trees; moss-covered stumps; a mini-wetland with log bridges over streams; and plenty of animal tracks. The marshy area has many flowers.

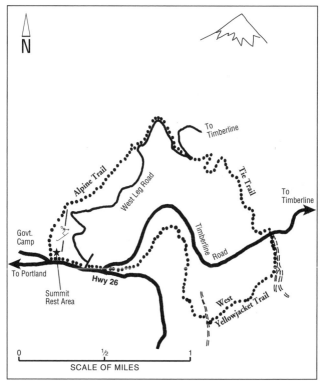

WEST LEG ROAD TO VIEWPOINT
Moderate (700 ft elevation gain, forest roads)
5½ miles roundtrip, 3–4 hours
Map: USGS, Mt Hood South Quadrangle

Description: This is a delightful hike to a clearcut near
Snowbunny Lodge with spectacular views of Mt Hood.
The early part of the hike is on Summit Ski Area and
Alpine Trail; the rest is on the old Timberline Road,
West Leg Road, or on forest roads with gentle grades.

Access: Park at the Summit Rest Area at the far (east)
end of the Government Camp business loop and follow
the service road up the left side of Summit Ski Area,
behind the Day Lodge, to the top of the chairlift.
Continue on the forest road to the left of the chairlift ter-
minal. This is the end of Alpine ski trail from Timberline
Lodge. Follow Alpine Trail for about ⅓ mile until you
can see paved West Leg Road (the old road to
Timberline Lodge) on the right, close to the trail. Turn
left onto West Leg Road and continue to climb gently for
½ mile to a left-hand bend where an unpaved forest road
takes off to the right, signed Tie Trail to Snowbunny
Lodge. The Tie Trail connects up with, and crosses, the
main road to Timberline Lodge. After crossing, continue
on the forest road towards Snowbunny Lodge and turn
sharply left onto another forest road about ¼ mile from
Timberline Road, signed to Viewpoint (the sign is high
on a tree on the left of the road). Continue on this road
for about ¾ mile to its end in an old clearcut on the left.
Turn left and climb up through the clearcut for the most
spectacular view. To return, retrace your steps, making
sure to make the correct turns at the intersections.

Features: This hike passes through some beautiful forest with tall, moss-festooned trees, and offers spectacular views of Mt Hood. The last section of the forest road, before the viewpoint, crosses many streams and their sound, and the bird calls, add to the tranquility of this hike. There are many flowers beside the streams. Keep an eye out for elk—or at least for their hoofprints. This is a comfortable hike to take when you would like to walk beside your companions because almost all of the hike is on forest roads.

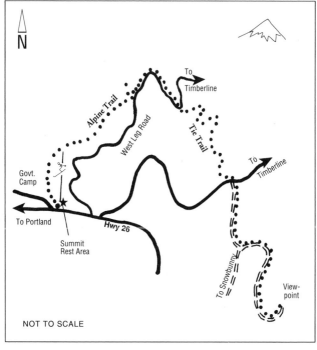

WIND LAKE
Moderate-to-Strenous (1,190 ft elevation gain; some steep and uneven terrain)
4½–6½ miles roundtrip (depending on the combination), 3½–4½ hours
Map: USGS, Government Camp Quadrangle

Description: A hike with spectacular views of Mt Hood and a beautiful lake as a goal. This hike works well as a loop from Government Camp, combining forest roads and a steep mountain bike trail. These trails are all part of the Ski Bowl Ski Area, except for the trail down to Wind Lake. This has become a popular mountain bike area in the summer. On trails that allow both hikers and mountain bikes, hikers should give way to bikes.

Access: From the Summit Rest Area at the far (east) end of the Government Camp business loop, go into Government Camp on the business loop and take the road to Ski Bowl East at Charlie's Mt View Restaurant. Cross the overpass, pass the Golden Poles Condominiums and cross the parking lot, skirting the summer fun area (can-am cars, trampoline and bungie jumping). Walk up to the Ski Bowl East Day Lodge and take the service road that heads west (right) from the Day Lodge and follow it under the Cascade chairlift and a rope-tow to the bottom of the Multorpor chairlift. From here, there are two options: the first, and easier, is to follow a combination of service road that leads you up to and along Skyline Road to the top of the Upper Bowl of Ski Bowl West. The second approach combines service roads and a mountain bike trail, and is shorter and prettier, but steeper. The decision does not need to be made until you reach the Warming Hut at the top of the main ski run on Ski Bowl West. To reach this, follow the upper service road over to Ski Bowl West from the bottom of Multorpor Chair, signed Low Road for mountain bikers, and gravelled most of the way. Then, either loop back to Ski Bowl East staying on the service road to the upper terminus of Multorpor chairlift, and continue on the service road, now Skyline Road, as it bends sharply to the right. Follow Skyline Road up and around the back of the hill to the top of the Upper Bowl of Ski Bowl. To take the shorter, steeper route, find the mountain bike trail above and to the right (east) of the Warming Hut, in the trees, and follow the bike trail up the left side of the Upper Bowl until it meets the Skyline Road. Continue uphill on this road for 100 yards and turn left onto a forest road, signed Wind Lake Trail for mountain bikers. The lake is about ½ mile down a gentle grade. To return, retrace your steps to the top of Ski Bowl and return down the Upper Bowl on the steep, rocky trail on the east side (right side facing downhill) of the bowl. Return to Ski Bowl East by the same service roads you came up on.

Continued on page 30

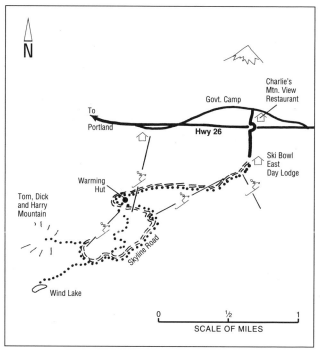

Features: The views on this hike are truly spectacular once you reach the top of the Upper Bowl of Ski Bowl West: Mt Hood to the north and the Salmon-Huckleberry Wilderness and Mt Jefferson to the south. Huckleberries are plentiful at the east edge of Ski Bowl in August, and mushrooms on the Wind Lake road in the fall. These trails are being used by mountain bikers, but not heavily. Wind Lake is about two acres, and though very attractive, is too shallow for fish or for swimming. The flat rocks on the north side make a perfect picnic site. Flowers are plentiful along the trails, and around the marshy area near the lake: beargrass, penstemon, anemones, paintbrush, marsh marigold, wild strawberries, yellow and blue violets, and shooting stars. Bunchberries carpet the slopes beside the steep trail down Upper Ski Bowl. Watch and listen for the shrill peeps of the pikas (rock rabbits) on the rock outcroppings on Upper Bowl.

Alternatives: 1) The ski lifts at Ski Bowl operate at weekends in the summer for the Alpine Slide and mountain bikers. Consider taking the lift to the top of Upper Bowl to make this a very gentle walk with very little elevation gain. **2)** To extend the hike and get an even better view, turn left (west) onto Skyline Road after returning from Wind Lake and continue up towards the top of the Upper Bowl Chairlift. At the last bend to the right before the top of the chairlift, find a faint trail that heads left (west). Follow this to the top of Tom, Dick and Harry Mountain, about ¼ mile.

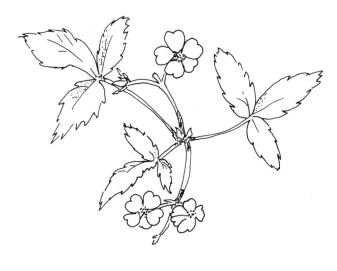

Wild Strawberry

WEST LEG ROAD–SUMMIT MEADOW–STILL CREEK LOOP
Moderate (easy hiking mostly on roads, 800 ft elevation gain)
6 mile loop, 2½–3½ hours
Map: USGS, Mt Hood South Quadrangle

Description: An appealing hike that loops up from the Summit Ski Area, over to Snowbunny sledding area, down to beautiful Summit Meadow and up Still Creek road and a portion of the old Barlow wagon trail. Most of the hike is on forest roads and trails; three ½ mile sections are on paved roads with some car traffic.

Access: Park at the Summit Rest Area at the far (east) end of the Government Camp business loop and follow the service road that goes up the left side of Summit Ski Area to the top of the chairlift. Continue on the forest road to the left of the lift. This is the end of Alpine Trail from Timberline Lodge. Continue up Alpine trail for about ⅓ mile until a paved road—West Leg Road—can be seen on the right close to the trail. Continue left up West Leg Road for ½ mile to a left-hand bend where an unpaved road takes off to the right, signed Tie Trail to Snowbunny Lodge. Follow the Tie Trail until it crosses the Timberline Road and continue on the forest road on the other side of the highway for about 1½ miles until it reaches Hwy 26, just after the Snowbunny sledding area. Cross Hwy 26 and walk ½ mile down Road #2656 towards Trillium Lake, to the bottom of the first hill. Where the road flattens out, there is an intersection on the right signed Still Creek Campground. Take this and follow the road round to the large open meadow, Summit Meadow. The road skirts the main meadow, passes the Pioneer Baby's grave on the left by the cabins, and comes to a junction. The left fork curls back to Trillium Lake. Continue straight to return to Hwy 26, through Still Creek Campground. Do not take the right loop around the campground, but continue straight until you see a trail junction, beside a noticeboard. This is Still Creek Trail, part of the old Barlow wagon trail. Continue up the trail, ignoring a side trail to the left, until it reaches the Forest Service cabins on Hwy 26, just opposite the Summit Rest Area.

Features: This hike offers great views of Mt Hood, quiet forest roads and a magnificent display of flowers in early summer in Summit Meadow—the site of one of the toll-gates on the Barlow Trail. Since this loop is a composite of several cross-country ski trails, some attention must be paid to following the map, or directions. It is is not far from the beaten track, however, so it is not hard to find your way. A good choice when you would like to walk beside your companions, not in single file. Short portions of the hike are on paved roads and car traffic on these sections is a possible hazard.

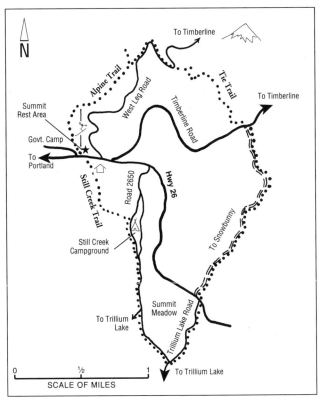

WEST OF GOVERNMENT CAMP

The trails to the west of Government Camp, with the exception of the popular Mirror Lake trail, are largely ignored. This is unfortunate because there are some exquisite trails in this area that are accessible to hikers of all ages and fitness levels. Some of the trails in this area have very little elevation gain or loss, so are not strenuous; most are through relatively open forest with streams providing added appeal. The Oregon Trail headed west through this area so it is soaked in history. In particular, the drama, triumphs, and sometimes tragedy, played out at Laurel Hill where the covered wagons were eased down a precipitous 200 ft slide by ropes wrapped around trees, make this area particularly interesting.

Some of the trails in this area have been made for cross-country skiing; some follow sections of the old Barlow Road wagon trails. The network of trails provides a variety of options for the hiker from very short walks to longer, more challenging hikes. The network also provides the opportunity to combine trails into longer hikes and interesting loops.

We describe some of the options and leave the rest up to your creativity. This is really a very beautiful area for hiking on mostly well-maintained trails, and gentle grades. The forest, wildflowers, streams, rhododendrons, and birds add to the beauty and enjoyment.

Directions to the trailhead are given from Summit Rest Area at the far (east) end of the Government Camp business loop and, where appropriate, from Rhododendron or Portland.

Trail to Little Zigzag Falls

PIONEER BRIDLE TRAIL

The Pioneer Bridle Trail (#795) extends 9 miles from the west end of Government Camp to Tollgate Campground. It follows the route of the old Barlow Road wagon trail and parts of it are probably actual portions of the old trail. The trail divides conveniently into two segments: Lower Pioneer Bridle Trail from the Kiwanis Camp Road to Tollgate Campground, and Upper Pioneer Bridle Trail from the Kiwanis Camp Road to the Glacier View Snopark. The upper segment involves more elevation gain than the lower, but is considerably more attractive.

UPPER PIONEER BRIDLE TRAIL
Moderate
4 miles one way, 2–3 hours; 8 miles roundtrip, 4–5 hours
Map: USGS, Government Camp Quadrangle

Description: A beautiful hike through second growth forest along portions of the old Barlow Road wagon trail. The hike works well as a one-way hike with car shuttle or as a roundtrip. There is about an 1,100 ft elevation gain if hiking from west to east, and loss if hiking from east to west. Generally, hiking uphill is more leisurely, so you have more time to enjoy the surroundings and spot the flowers, and other interesting features along the way.

Access: To hike the trail *uphill* (from west to east): Find the trailhead on the north (mountain) side of Hwy 26 at its junction with the Kiwanis Camp Road. The junction is between mileposts 48 and 49, 5.4 miles west of the Summit Rest Area at the far end of the Government Camp business loop and 4.1 miles east of Rhododendron. The trail is fairly flat at first, then climbs steadily with some relatively flat sections interspersed with steeper sections. The grade is mostly quite easy. At one point, the trail passes under the old road in a tunnel. At another point, it comes close to Hwy 26, then continues up the hill (ignore the trail to the left here). As the

36

trail begins to flatten out after the uphill grade, there will be a fork to the right to the old highway. Go straight at the fork for about ¾ mile to the trailhead, following the blue diamond-shaped ski trail markers in the trees, and ignoring a fork on the left to Enid Lake.

To hike the trail *downhill* (from east to west): From the Summit Rest Area at the far (east) end of the Government Camp business loop, drive 1.5 miles west on Hwy 26 and turn right (north) onto road #522 between mileposts 52 and 53 or almost opposite the west entrance to Ski Bowl. There is ample parking beside the barrier about 200 yards from Hwy 26. Take Pioneer Bridle Trail (#795) to the left (west) and when it divides in about 100 yards, take the right fork. The trail is well-marked and there are blue diamond-shaped ski trail signs high on the trees. Ignore a junction on the right signed to Enid Lake, and one further on on the left that leads back to the old highway. The trail then drops steadily in a few loops, comes close to Hwy 26, and passes under the old highway through a tunnel. Continue on for 2.3 miles, to the trailhead at the junction of Hwy 26 and the Kiwanis Camp Road.

Continued on page 38

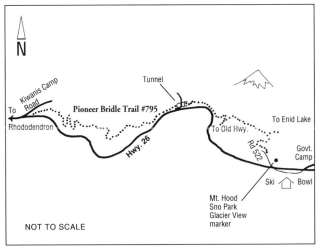

NOT TO SCALE

37

Features: The rhododendrons on this trail are spectacular in early summer. For moss lovers, this trail is a must before everything dries out in late July: moss carpets much of the forest floor and the rocks. The steepest part of the trail lies beside a section of the old wagon road where the wagons had to be winched down the slopes with ropes. Further up, the trail follows a well-preserved section of the old road. There is also an abandoned mine shaft beside the trail—recognizable by the fence around it. This is a perfect hike for a hot day because it is cool and shady under the trees—but not in any way dark or dank. There are lots of flowers in spring and early summer. Listen for the peep of the pikas (rock rabbits) where the trail crosses a rockfall.

Wooden Horse Trough, Tollgate Campground

LOWER PIONEER BRIDLE TRAIL

Easy
4.6 miles one way, 2–3 hours; 9.2 miles roundtrip,
    4–5 hours
Map: USGS, Government Camp Quadrangle

The main attraction of this segment of the Pioneer Bridle
Trail (#795) is its historic interest as part of the old
Barlow Road wagon trail. It is also easily accessible to
Camp Creek and Tollgate Campgrounds. The constant
traffic noise from Hwy 26 is intrusive, however, so we
do not recommend this hike for those seeking a quiet
walk, and only describe it briefly.

Access: The upper trailhead is on the south side of Hwy
26 at its intersection with the Kiwanis Camp Road
between mileposts 48 and 49, 5 miles west of
Government Camp and 4.1 miles east of Rhododendron.
The lower trailhead is at the reconstructed tollgate at the
Rest Area on the right (south) side of Hwy 26, ½ mile east
of Rhododendron and 9 miles west of Government Camp.

Features: This section of the Pioneer Bridle Trail passes
through some beautiful sections of forest. Look for a
moss-covered wooden horse trough beside the trail as it
passes through Tollgate Campground, just west of the
Rest Area.

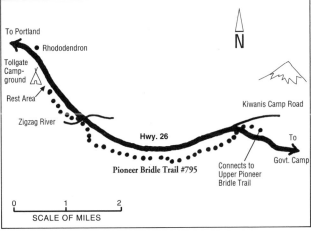

39

ENID LAKE TO LAUREL HILL
**Moderate (hiking mostly flat, one steep section;
  trail sometimes indistinct)**
3 miles roundtrip from Enid Lake
Map: USGS, Government Camp Quadrangle

Description: This hike combines history with mystery: history because the trail follows the old Barlow wagon road from the east end of Government Camp to the infamous Laurel Hill, where the pioneers had to ease their wagons down a precipitous grade; mystery because this trail is seldom used and is sometimes indistinct—though signed at crucial points. The hike does entail crossing Hwy 26, but the traffic is rarely so constant that this poses a problem or hazard—the exception to this would be in the late afternoon on weekends. Much of the trail is through fairly dense young forest which gives it almost a tunnel-like feel, adding to the sense of mystery. This is not a hike for the person who needs the well-trodden path and lots of company. It is a hike for the person who is looking for a challenge and is interested in the history of the area.

Access: From the Summit Rest Area at the far (east) end of the Government Camp business loop, drive 1.5 miles west on Hwy 26 and turn right (north) onto Road #522 between mileposts 52 and 53—almost opposite the west entrance to Ski Bowl. There is ample parking about 200 yards from Hwy 26, beside the barrier. The trail is easily seen on the right from the road and is signed Pioneer Bridle Trail #795. Follow this to the left (west) and when it divides (about 100 yards), take the left fork marked "Barlow Road". The right fork is the Pioneeer Bridle Trail and is marked with blue diamonds high on the trees. The old Barlow Road is initially easy to follow but soon becomes somewhat indistinct and passes through a boggy section where the trail disappears for a short distance. It picks up the other side of an area rich with skunk cabbage at about 10 o'clock and once again becomes firm and dry. After a short distance, it emerges at the old paved highway and picks up again diagonally and to the left, at about 9 o'clock, near the beginning of a gravel road. The entrance to this section of the trail is narrow and overgrown, so look carefully. A sign "Original Wagon Road" on a tree near the entrance will tell you that you are on the right track. Follow the trail until it crosses a power line service road and picks up directly opposite. The trail next emerges from the forest at the top of a high bank above Hwy 26. Follow the narrow path to the left, hugging the edge of the trees, and cross Hwy 26 (carefully!). Once across, follow the old paved highway to the right and about 100 yards from Hwy 26 watch carefully for a narrow trail that takes off to the left where the banks starts. Proceed uphill on the trail for 20 yards, then turn left and follow the trail for about ½ mile. The only tricky spot is where the trail comes to a partial clearing and picks up almost directly opposite, again signed "Original Wagon Road". The trail crosses the old highway for the last time, resumes on the opposite side, and soon joins the new trail to Laurel Hill from Hwy 26. At this junction, take a right and you are soon at the top of Laurel Hill chute where the wagons were lowered on ropes. There is an interesting Forest Service interpretive marker at the top of the rocky chute.

Continued on page 42

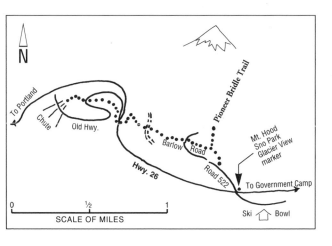

Features: This trail, perhaps more than any other in this area, makes the pioneers' journey come alive. The narrowness and unevenness of the trail and the canopy of trees overhead all heighten the effect. There are relatively few flowers in this part of the forest but the moss that covers segments of the trail makes it green and lush. The early part of the forest, near Enid Lake, is much more open and has spectacular trees, and abundant huckleberries. The views down Zigzag valley towards Portland, from the top of the chute, are magnificent.

Mountain Ash

LITTLE ZIGZAG FALLS
Easy
½ mile each way; ½ – ¾ hour roundtrip
Map: USGS, Government Camp Quadrangle

Description: A jewel of a short hike (#759C) suitable for all ages and all fitness levels. The trail follows the Little Zigzag River and ends at the Little Zigzag Falls. The trail is very well-maintained, and you'll encounter only a small elevation gain.

Access: The trailhead is at the east (far) end of the Kiwanis Camp Road. From the Summit Rest Area at the east (far) end of the Government Camp business loop, take Hwy 26 west 5.4 miles and turn right (north) onto the Kiwanis Camp Road #39, just after milepost 48. From Rhododendron, go east on Hwy 26 4.1 miles, and turn left (north) onto the Kiwanis Camp Road. The trailhead is 2.3 miles from Hwy 26, on the left, at the end of the paved road.

Features: This is a very peaceful and quiet hike through a beautiful, open forest with the music of the river in the background. The falls, though relatively small, are spectacular. Flowers are plentiful in the spring, some mushrooms in the fall.

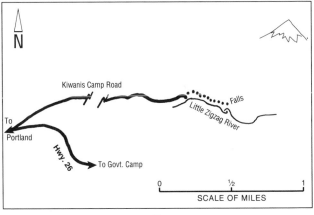

LAUREL HILL CHUTE TRAIL
Easy (one flight of steps; gentle grade)
1.0 mile round-trip; ¾ hour
Map: USGS, Government Camp Quadrangle

Description: A short, new trail (#795A) that climbs to the top of Laurel Hill—reputedly the section of the old Barlow wagon road where the pioneers had to ease their wagons down a steep, rocky chute by braking their descent with ropes wound around trees. The trail is well-marked and well-graded. The history adds flavor to the hike, and the views are worth the short climb.

Access: The trailhead is on the south side of Hwy 26, 6.4 miles east of Rhododendron and 3.2 miles west of the Summit Rest Area at the far (east) end of the Government Camp business loop, and is well-marked by an historical site sign. From Hwy 26, the trail climbs up to the old highway by a flight of steps, follows the road to the right past an interesting interpretive plaque, then takes off on the left and climbs 0.4 miles in gentle loops, passing two forks—both on the right. Ignore both of them. After the second fork, the trail curves to the left to reach the top of the chute. Return by the same trail. Accessibility and historic interest have made this a popular trail, but there is usually room to park at the trailhead.

Features: There is some controversy as to whether the rocky chute at Laurel Hill was really the site of the infamous, precipitous chute, so feared by the pioneers because of the toll it took of wagons and livestock. Whether or not it is the exact site, this short hike gives a fascinating glimpse into the past, and makes the feats of the pioneers all the more impressive. The views down the Zigzag valley, towards Portland, are superb. The name Laurel comes from the rhododendrons that belong to the laurel family and grow in abundance in the area.

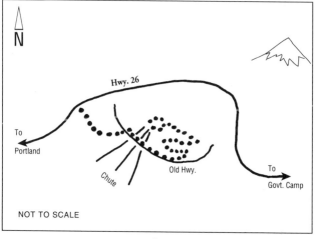

ENID LAKE TO LITTLE ZIGZAG FALLS
Moderate (mostly gentle grade)
4½ miles; 2½–3 hours
Map: USGS, Government Camp Quadrangle

Description: This hike takes you along segments of the old Barlow wagon route, and the old Mt Hood highway. Little Zigzag Falls is a short distance from the old highway and makes a charming destination for the hike. The portion of the hike that is on a trail is well-maintained and has mostly gentle grades. The portions on the old highway are paved and flat. Unlike the Forest Service's named and numbered hikes this is a composite of portions of several hikes, so some care is needed in following the map and instructions.

Access: From the Summit Rest Area at the far (east) end of the Government Camp business loop, drive 1.5 miles west on Hwy 26 and turn right (north) onto Road #522 between mileposts 52 and 53—almost opposite the west entrance to Ski Bowl. There is ample parking on the right about 200 yds from the highway, beside the barrier. The trail comes very close to the road at this point and can easily be seen on the right from the parking area. Follow this to the left (west) and when it divides (about 100 yards), take the right fork, signed Pioneer Bridle Trail, and marked with blue diamond-shaped ski trail signs high on the trees. Continue past a junction on the right after about ⅓ mile, leading to Enid Lake, and a junction on the left that leads up to the old highway after another ½ mile. The trail then drops steadily in a few loops and comes very close to Hwy 26. Continue on until the trail goes through a tunnel under the old highway. Just before the tunnel you can see the old paved highway at the right. Take the old highway to the right for about ¼ mile and find the trailhead to Little Zigzag Falls on the right, just after a barrier. Return the same way.

Features: This trail starts in beautiful, open forest with abundant huckleberry bushes (berries in late August), follows parts of one of the old Barlow wagon roads, and continues past streams that make their own wetland environment. The forest changes constantly in character throughout the hike as the amount of water varies. Wildflowers and birds abound. The short hike to Little Zigzag Falls adds an extra special bonus to this lovely hike.

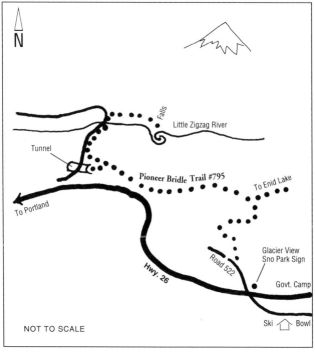

HIDDEN LAKE

**Moderate (mostly gentle grade or almost flat; one
short steeper section)**
4 miles roundtrip; 2–2½ hours
Map: USGS, Government Camp Quadrangle

Description: An easy hike on a well-maintained trail
(#779) to a small lake east of Zigzag Canyon in the Mt
Hood Wilderness. The trail starts with a series of switch-
backs, then levels off for the rest of the way, and wends
through mostly open forest. Apart from one fairly steep
(short) section, the grade is very easy. This is the first
portion of a trail that continues to climb steadily to meet
the round-the-mountain (Timberline) trail west of Little
Zigzag Canyon. Hidden Lake is not suitable for camping
or swimming. Since part of this hike is in the Mt Hood
Wilderness, remember to sign in at the registration box
as you pass it on the trail.

Access: The trailhead is on the left (north) side of the
Kiwanis Camp Road. From the Summit Rest Area at the
far (east) end of the Government Camp business loop,
take Hwy 26 west 5.4 miles towards Portland, and turn
right (north) onto the Kiwanis Camp Road, beween
mileposts 48 and 49. From Rhododendron, go east on
Hwy 26 4.1 miles, and turn left onto the Kiwanis Camp
Road. The trailhead is 2 miles from Hwy 26, on the left
(north) side of the road. Follow the trail for 2 miles until
it dips down and crosses a small stream—the outflow
from the lake. The lake is easily visible on the right.
Return the same way. For a longer hike, continue on the
main trail which joins the round-the-mountain trail
(Timberline Trail #600 and Pacific Crest Trail #2000)
after another 2½ miles. Turn right (east) to reach
Timberline Lodge.

Features: Impressive banks of rhododendrons line the trail and are spectacular in late June or early July; great views, over to Laurel Hill and Tom, Dick and Harry Mountain after the initial zigzags. There are yellow violets, beargrass, and bunchberries after the snow melts in spring, and a luxurient growth of skunk cabbage beside the lake. Moss carpets the forest floor, rocks, and stumps along parts of the trail. This is a gentle hike, suitable for all ages and hiking abilities.

Cat's Ear Lily

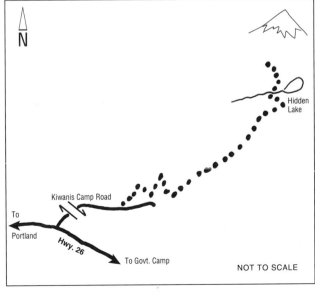

MIRROR LAKE AND TOM, DICK & HARRY VIEWPOINT

Easy to Mirror Lake; moderate to Viewpoint
3.2 miles roundtrip to Mirror Lake, 2–2½ hours;
6.4 miles roundtrip to viewpoint, 3½–4½ hours
Map: USGS, Government Camp Quadrangle

Description: A very gradual, well-graded trail (#664) that starts at a waterfall, then climbs 1.6 miles to Mirror Lake in gentle zigzags. This is the most popular trail in the area—for good reasons. The trail is very well maintained, easy to follow and the grade is gentle. When the water is still, Mt Hood is mirrored in the lake. Small beaches make swimming enticing in hot weather. The lake is stocked although the fish are small. There are 6 campsites at the southwest end of the lake. Usually the area has lots of children, dogs, and large groups, and it is showing signs of use. If the parking area is crowded, consider one of the other trails in the area. The additional 1.6 miles to the viewpoint on Tom, Dick and Harry Mountain is well worth the effort.

Access: The trailhead is on the south side of Hwy 26 beween mileposts 51 and 52, 2.2 miles west of the Summit Rest Area at the far (east) end of the Government Camp business loop. There is usually ample parking beside the road. The trailhead is marked by a footbridge that crosses Camp Creek just above Yocum Falls. The trail zigzags gently up to the lake, and forks just before it reaches the lake. Both forks lead to the 0.4-mile trail that loops around the lake. The right fork also leads to the trail up to Tom, Dick & Harry Mountain. This trail leaves the loop trail just after it reaches the lake and climbs gradually but steadily to a rocky viewpoint on one of the three summits of Tom Dick & Harry Mountain.

Features: Spectacular views of Mt Hood reflected in Mirror Lake, a scenic and comfortable picnic site, a swimming beach and campsites all add to the attractiveness of this lovely hike. The trail to the lake passes through a magnificent grove of Douglas fir trees and opens onto a rockslide where you can hear the bleating of the little rock rabbits (pikas). Lots of rhododendrons in early summer, and a sprinkling of other flowers later.

Optional Add-on: Continue on up Tom, Dick and Harry Mountain for a longer hike. The extra distance (1.6 miles to the viewpoint) is well worth the effort because the additional elevation brings spectacular views north to Mt Hood and Government Camp, west over the Zigzag valley, and south to the Salmon-Huckleberry Wilderness. There are also more flowers on this section of the trail, and huckleberries in the fall. The well-marked trail ends at the first summit.

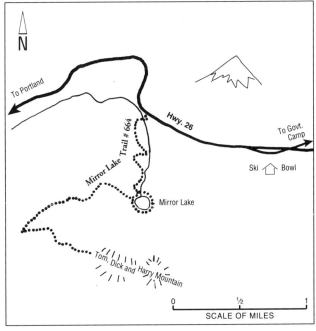

TOM, DICK & HARRY MOUNTAIN LOOP
Strenuous (1,666 ft elevation gain; trail indistinct and uneven in places)
6 mile loop, 3½–4½ hours
Map: USGS, Government Camp Quadrangle

Description: A spectacular loop hike that includes Mirror Lake, the three summits of Tom, Dick and Harry Mountain and Ski Bowl. Mt Hood towers to the north, flanked by the Salmon-Huckleberry Wilderness and Mt Jefferson, Three Sisters, and Broken Top to the south. The hike starts on the Mirror Lake trail and finishes at Ski Bowl so it requiries a short (0.6 mile) car shuttle or hike along Hwy 26. This hike is ranked as strenuous because there is appreciable elevation gain, the trail is indistinct for part of the way, and the trail down Upper Ski Bowl is steep and uneven.

Access: From the Summit Rest Area at the far (east) end of the Government Camp business loop, drive 2.2 miles west on Hwy 26 to the trailhead for Mirror Lake on the left (south) side of the road beside the creek, between mileposts 51 and 52. The trail starts on the far side of the creek, over a footbridge. Follow the trail 1.6 miles to Mirror Lake, take the right fork just before the lake, and the next right fork signed to Tom, Dick & Harry Mountain. The viewpoint, at one of the three summits of Tom, Dick & Harry Mountain, is 1.6 miles further on a well-maintained trail that climbs at a steady grade. After the viewpoint, the trail becomes quite indistinct, especially where it goes over rocks. If you stay just below the ridge, you won't go wrong. Keep following the ridge as it climbs to the third summit of Tom, Dick & Harry Mountain—the western limit of Ski Bowl runs. From there, the trail follows a ski trail to the top of the Upper Bowl chairlift. When it joins a service road by a green metal building, just before the last bend before the top of the chairlift, turn right and follow the road down for about ¼ mile to where the top of the Upper Bowl is close to the road. Take the steep, Upper Bowl mountain bike trail down the east side (right side facing down) of the Upper Bowl and continue down the signed mountain bike trails to the Day Lodge. **For a car shuttle,** leave one car at Ski Bowl, and the other at the Mirror Lake trailhead. If you don't have a shuttle, walk west (left) down Hwy 26 for 0.6 miles to the trailhead.

Features: This is one of the most spectacular hikes in Oregon. The views are breathtaking in every direction and the flowers are abundant. This is not the hike for someone who prefers the well-trodden path, however, and it requires clear visibility. Be sure to yield to mountain bikes on all roads and trails that are marked for their use at Ski Bowl—bikes have right of way.

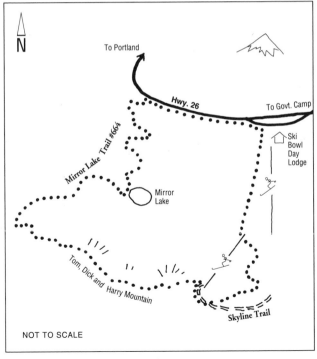

NORTH OF GOVERNMENT CAMP

All of the trails to the north of Government Camp involve appreciable elevation gain, but reward the effort with spectacular views. Two ski trails, Glade and Alpine, connect Government Camp and Timberline Lodge and are used in winter by both downhill and cross-country skiers. The elevation gain going up and loss coming down is about 2,100 ft, about 500 ft less if you go only to the top of Alpine Trail. We have chosen to describe them as three separate hikes: Glade Trail alone, Alpine Trail alone, and both combined into a loop. We have also included them in the Timberline Lodge section to provide information about accessing them from the Lodge. Both Glade and Alpine Trails work well as a one-way hike with car shuttle—starting either from Government Camp or from Timberline Lodge.

The other trail in this section, the West Fork Falls–Alpine Loop, covers some of the same area and also involves an appreciable elevation gain. It too offers spectacular views and adds in a secluded waterfall and stream, and a lovely section through the forest.

You can access all of the trails in this section from Government Camp; instructions for finding the trails use the Summit Rest Area at the far (east) end of the Government Camp business loop as a reference.

West Fork Falls

GLADE TRAIL FROM GOVERNMENT CAMP
Moderate (2,100 ft elevation gain)
3 miles one way, 2-3 hours; 6 miles roundtrip,
3½–4½ hours
Map: USGS, Mt Hood South Quadrangle

Description: A steady but mostly gradual climb from Government Camp to Timberline Lodge on a trail (#661) used for downhill and cross-country skiing in winter. Spectacular views of Mt Hood are a fitting reward for the effort. This hike works well as a one-way hike with car shuttle, or as a roundtrip.

Car Shuttle: Leave one car in Government Camp, or at the Summit Rest Area at the far (east) end of the Government Camp business loop, and the other at Timberline Lodge.

Access: Park in Government Camp or at the Summit Rest Area at the far (east) end of the Government Camp business loop. If you park at the Summit Rest Area, follow the loop highway west to Government Camp village and turn up the road to the west (left) of Huckleberry Inn, on the north side of the loop highway. The first ¼ mile is paved and passes some of the original cabins interspersed with new large and small homes. When the paved road ends, follow the well-marked trail that heads more or less straight up to Timberline Lodge. The trail is quite faint initially but soon opens up. Ignore service roads that intersect with the main trail about ¼ mile from the start of the trail. The main trail goes under a power line and turns right. Continue up the trail for about 1½ miles until it joins a service road beside a power line. Continue up the service road and turn right just above the bottom end of the Magic Mile Chairlift. Timberline Lodge is straight ahead. Return the same way, or make a loop by returning to Government Camp down Alpine Trail (see page 58) or see Alpine and Glade Trail Loop (page 60).

Features: This hike provides a satisfying workout with fantastic views along the way. Flowers are plentiful, especially in early summer, and mushrooms abound, lower down, in the fall. Listen for the whirr of the mountain grouse, and keep an eye out for deer. No one says you have to make it to the top—if you don't feel like going the whole way, find a spot with a great view and enjoy!

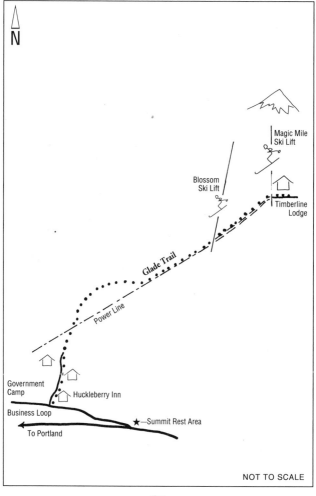

ALPINE TRAIL FROM GOVERNMENT CAMP
Moderate (2,100 ft elevation gain)
3-miles one way with car shuttle, 2–3 hours;
    6 miles roundtrip, 3½–4½ hours
Map: USGS, Mt Hood South Quadrangle

Description: A steady climb with one very steep section on a ski trail (#660) that connects Government Camp and Timberline Lodge. Spectacular views, abundant flowers and solitude are a fitting reward. Mountain bikers are using this trail more but it is still very peaceful. This hike works well as a one-way hike with car shuttle, or as a roundtrip.

Car Shuttle: Leave one car in Government Camp, or at the Summit Rest Area at the far (east) end of the Government Camp business loop, and the other at Timberline Lodge.

Access: Park at the Summit Rest Area at the far (east) end of the Government Camp business loop and follow the service road on the left of the Summit Ski area, behind the Day Lodge, to the top of the chairlift. Continue on the forest road to the left of the chairlift—now Alpine Trail—for about 2 miles to the bottom of Blossom Chairlift. The trail is actually an old rutted service road, rather than a trail, and is quite steep in sections; the steepest part is Mazama Hill. From the bottom of Blossom Chairlift, continue up the service road, under the chairs, for about 100 yards and turn right onto the steep service road that leads up to the Magic Mile Chairlift, and Timberline Lodge. Once you have reached the bottom of Blossom Chairlift, Timberline Lodge is only another ½ mile and 500 ft climb. Return the same way, or make a loop by returning to Government Camp down Glade Trail (see page 56) or see Alpine and Glade Trail Loop (page 60).

Features: This hike, like Glade Trail, provides a satisfying workout with fantastic views along the way. Timberline Lodge is a perfect turnaround point since it offers a variety of enticing ways to reward yourself for the climb. Alpine Trail is quite secluded and peaceful and often has a glorious display of beargrass in early summer—as well as many other flowers. Listen for the whirr of the mountain grouse, and watch for deer.

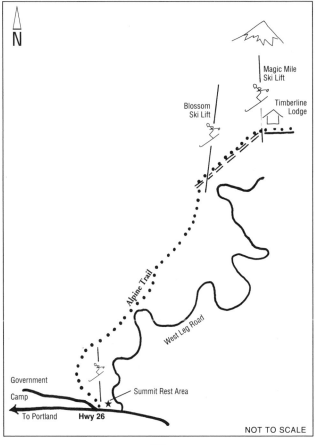

ALPINE AND GLADE TRAIL LOOP
Moderate (1,600 ft elevation gain and loss, some steep sections)
5.5-mile loop, 3½–4½ hours
Map: USGS, Mt Hood South Quadrangle

Description: This loop follows ski trails that link Timberline Lodge with Government Camp. The loop can be hiked clockwise (up Glade #661, down Alpine, #660) or counterclockwise (up Alpine, down Glade). The trails are quite different—Glade is wider, and more open; Alpine is narrower, steeper, and more secluded. Since these are ski trails in winter, they are not signed or maintained as hiking trails. They are easy to follow, however, and for the most part, have a good surface.

Access: 1) *Counterclockwise:* Park at the Summit Rest Area at the far (east) end of the Government Camp business loop and follow the service road on the left of the Summit Ski Area, behind the Day Lodge, to the top of the chairlift. Continue on the forest road to the left of the chairlift terminus—now Alpine Trail— for about 2 miles, to the bottom of Blossom Chairlift. The trail is actually an old rutted forest road, rather than a trail, and is quite steep in some sections; the steepest section is Mazama Hill. From the bottom of Blossom Chairlift, continue up the service road, under the lift, for about 100 yards and turn left downhill onto broad, open Glade Trail—initially a rough service road. Follow the road until you reach a T-junction and see a large orange sign for Glade Trail to the right. Follow this to the right to Government Camp, ignoring the service roads that intersect with the trail. The only difficult intersection is just above the village where the trail turns to the left under the powerline. A service road continues straight.

2) *Clockwise:* From the Summit Rest Area at the (east) end of Government Camp, follow the loop highway west to Government Camp village. Turn up the road to the west (left) of Huckleberry Inn, on the north side of the loop highway. The first ¼ mile is paved and passes some of the original cabins interspersed with new large and small homes. When the paved road ends, follow the well-marked trail that heads more or less straight up towards Timberline Lodge. The trail is quite narrow initially but soon opens up. Ignore service roads that intersect with the main trail about ¼ mile from the start of the trail. The main trail goes under the power line and turns right. Continue up the trail for about 1½ miles until it joins a service road beside the power line. Continue up the service road until it goes under Blossom Chairlift. Turn right under the chairlift to follow the chairs to the lower terminus—the top of Alpine Trail is just below, and to the right. The trail is not signed, but is quite obvious. Follow Alpine Trail down to the Summit Rest Area.

Continued on page 62

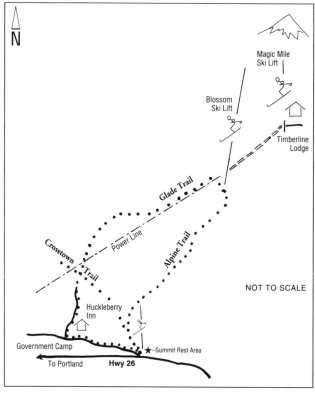

Features: Magnificent views of Mt Hood to the North and the Salmon-Huckleberry Wilderness and Mt Jefferson to the south. Both trails are in the full sun and can be hot. Flowers are plentiful on both trails; beargrass can blanket Mazama Hill. Listen for the whirr of the mountain grouse, and watch for deer. From the bottom of Blossom Chairlift, it is only about ½ mile and 500 ft up to Timberline Lodge and a great meal, or drink!

Alternative: A recently-built trail, Crosstown Trail (#755), which loops around the top of Government Camp village, offers an attractive alternative way to complete this loop, especially if hiking counterclockwise. The trail crosses Glade Trail just below the intersection of the powerline and Glade Trail (see map). Turn left (east) onto the new trail to return to Summit Ski Area and Summit Rest Area.

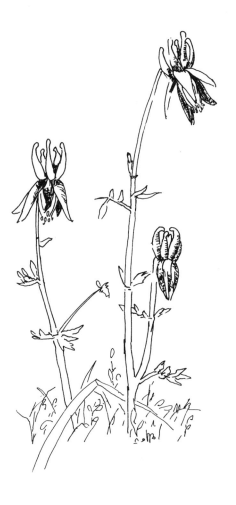

Columbine

WEST FORK FALLS–ALPINE TRAIL LOOP
Moderate (1,600 ft elevation gain)
6 mile loop, 4–5 hours
Map: USGS, Mt Hood South Quadrangle

Description: This hike works well as a loop from Government Camp, with the falls as the main destination. A perfect half-day hike, or a leisurely day hike with opportunities to linger along the way. Uphill grades are mostly gentle. Most of the hike is on forest trails or roads, part is on a relatively quiet paved road—West Leg Road, the old road to Timberline Lodge. The West Fork Falls Trail is not signed or maintained by the Forest Service. Since this loop consists of several trails and portions of forest and paved roads, exercise care in following the instructions or map.

Access: Park at the Summit Rest Area at the far (east) end of the Government Camp business loop and follow the service road up the left side of Summit Ski Area, behind the Day Lodge, to the top of the chairlift. Continue on the forest road to the left of the lift. This is the end of Alpine ski trail from Timberline Lodge. Continue up Alpine trail for about ⅓ mile until you can see a paved road—West Leg Road—on the right, close to the trail. Continue left up West Leg Road for about ½ mile to a left-hand bend where an unpaved road takes off to the right, signed as the Tie Trail to Snowbunny Lodge. Follow the Tie Trail for about 1 mile over Still Creek and down a gentle grade. The trail junction for the West Fork Falls Trail is not well-marked; look for a blue diamond-shaped ski trail marker on a tree on the left about a mile from the start of the Tie Trail. The trail junction is about 50 yards further, on the left, and is marked by a small pile of stones. There is also a trail entrance on the right of the Tie Trail, opposite the trail junction for West Fork Falls. The falls are about 0.6 miles up the trail. At the falls, the trail crosses the stream and follows it on the right bank passing three sets of falls that join the stream. The trail then follows and crosses a dry streambed before turning sharply to the left at a large fallen tree and continuing uphill until it crosses a steep service road, and becomes more indistinct. The trail curves round to join the service road and follows it up the last short pitch to join West Leg Road. Follow West Leg Road to the right, past the bottom of Pucci Chairlift, until you can see a second lift (Blossom) down to the left of the road. Follow the service road down to the chairlift and find the start of unsigned Alpine trail just below the lift. Follow the rutted Alpine Trail to Summit Rest Area.

Continued on page 66

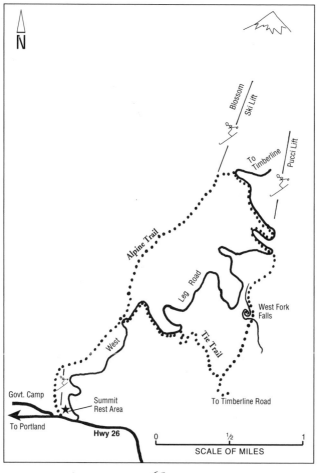

Features: This hike offers spectacular views of Mt Hood, a hidden and almost unknown falls and delightful mountain stream, flowers in the summer (especially by the stream), and mushrooms in the fall. The varied terrain and mix of open trails and forest—and the solitude—make this a particularly attractive hike. The hike can be shortened by driving up West Leg Road and parking at the start of the Tie Trail, or by walking down West Leg Road when the falls trail meets the paved road. It can be lengthened by continuing up West Leg Road to Timberline Lodge.

Shaggy Mane Mushrooms (Cuprinus Comatus)

SHORT DISTANCE FROM GOVERNMENT CAMP

Many hikes are available within a short distance of
Government Camp and Timberline Lodge. We have
selected a few because they are particularly interesting,
or because they are relatively short and suitable for all
ages and fitness levels. All require a drive from
Government Camp or Timberline Lodge. Directions to
the trailhead are given from the Summit Rest Area at the
far (east) end of the Government Camp business loop
and, where appropriate, from Portland or
Rhododendron.

Lost Creek Nature Trail

VEDA LAKE
Easy (short hike, 600 ft elevation gain)
2.2 miles roundtrip, 2–2½ hours
Map: USGS, Government Camp Quadrangle

Description: A beautiful trail (#673) to an attractive small lake suitable for swimming and fishing. An ideal choice for those seeking a shorter hike with a spectacular view of Mt Hood. The trail is well-maintained and well-graded. The trail starts with a modest uphill grade, levels out, then drops to the lake. Most of the elevation gain is on the return as the trail climbs back from the lake. The road to the trailhead is quite rough, but passable for most passenger cars.

Access: From the Summit Rest Area at the far (east) end of the Government Camp business loop, go east on Hwy 26 and take the Mt Hood National Forest Still Creek Campground exit on the right (#2650), ½ mile from the Rest Area. The road loops through the campground—keep going straight when it loops back—and continues to a large open meadow, Summit Meadow. Near the beginning of the fenced meadow, at a junction, take the right fork and continue to a 4-way intersection after ½ mile. Keep straight ahead on the Sherar Burn Road #2613. This road begins with a fairly good surface but deteriorates and becomes narrower and rocky in places, but still passable to most passenger cars. The trailhead and parking is 3½ miles up the Sherar Burn Road, on the left at the Fir Tree Campground. The trail begins on the right (north) side of the road, across from the parking area and is marked by a sign post. The trail climbs initially, then levels off before dropping in gentle zigzags to the lake.

Features: This trail offers an exceptional view of Mt Hood, a beautiful open mixed forest and plentiful wildflowers—lupine, paintbrush, twin flower, penstemon, lilies, and rhododendrons. The three-acre lake has become the home to Eastern Brook trout since Vern Rogers and Dave Donaldson introduced them in 1917. The name Veda comes from the combination of their first names. Enjoy a swim before heading back up the trail. A great site for camping, picnicing, and swimming.

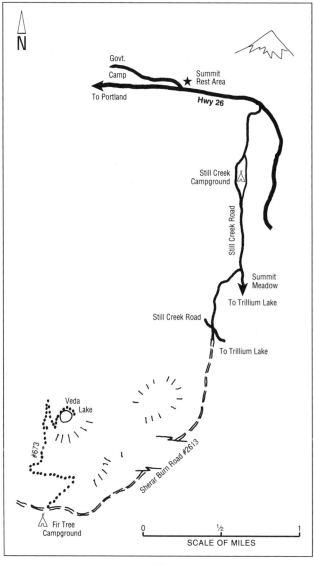

JACKPOT MEADOWS

Easy to Salmon River Bridge, moderate to Jackpot Meadows

2 miles roundtrip to Salmon River Bridge, 1–1½ hours; 5½ miles roundtrip to Jackpot Meadows, 2½–3½ hours

Maps: USGS, Wolf Peak and Mt Hood South Quadrangles

Description: A peaceful hike on a well-maintained trail that can be lengthened or shortened as desired. The trail descends gently for the first mile until it crosses the Salmon River. After crossing the Salmon River Bridge, the trail climbs steadily for 1¾ miles to Road #240, and beyond, to Jackpot Meadows.

Access: From the Summit Rest Area at the far (east) end of the Government Camp business loop, follow Hwy 26 for 1.8 miles east and turn right at the Trillium Lake sign (#2656). After 1.8 miles, just past the entrance to the Trillium Lake campground, turn left onto Road #2656 at a sign for the Salmon River trailhead. After 1.2 miles, bear right and follow a gravel road (#309) for 2.6 miles. Park at a pullout on the right beside the trailheads for Jackpot Meadows (#492) and Salmon River (#742).

Features: Beargrass, moss, and lichen-covered rocks and logs, and an avenue of hemlock and Douglas fir line this peaceful, remote trail. Huckleberries abound near the Salmon River. Beautiful vistas of Mt Hood can be seen as the trail climbs out of the valley beyond the Salmon River Bridge. A perfect hike when you want to get away from the crowds.

Clintonia

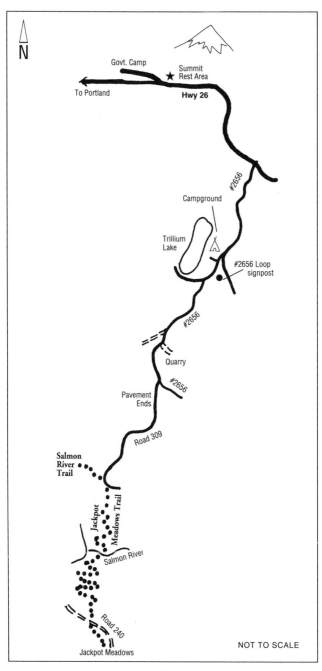

N

Govt. Camp

Summit
Rest Area

Hwy 26

To Portland

#2656

Campground

Trillium Lake

#2656 Loop
signpost

#2656

Quarry

#2656

Pavement
Ends

Road 309

**Salmon
River
Trail**

Jackpot
Meadows Trail

Salmon River

Road 240

Jackpot Meadows

NOT TO SCALE

73

EUREKA PEAK
Moderate (1,000 ft elevation gain)
4 miles roundtrip, 2–3 hours
Map: USGS, Government Camp Quadrangle

Description: The trail is about 2 miles each way—steadily uphill in one direction, down the other—and links two unpaved roads, Still Creek Road and Sherar Burn Road. There are a few relatively steep pitches, but mostly the trail has a comfortable grade. This is a recently reopened trail, not well-known to many, but likely to become increasingly used by hikers and mountain bikers as it becomes discovered. The hike can be extended by walking in either direction along Sherar Burn Road at the south end of the trail. The Sherar Burn Road trailhead is not well-marked, however. Take a good bearing so you don't miss the entrance.

Access: From the Summit Rest Area at the far (east) end of the Government Camp business loop, go east on Hwy 26 and take the Mt Hood National Forest Still Creek Campground exit on the right (Rd. #2650) ½ mile from the Rest Area. The road loops through the campground—keep straight when it loops back—and continues to a large open meadow, Summit Meadow. Near the beginning of the meadow, at a junction, take the right fork and continue to a 4-way intersection after ½ mile. Take the first (sharp) right road (Still Creek Road #2612) and follow this for 2.4 miles on a crushed rock road with some potholes. The trailhead takes off from the left (south) side of the road, and is marked by a small pile of stones and a temporary trail sign on a tree. It is not obvious, however, so watch your odometer. The road is wide enough to park on the edge.

Features: A perfect hike when the wild rhododendrons and beargrass are blooming, usually mid June to early July. Soon after leaving the trailhead, the trail crosses a pretty stream, and makes one zig before heading relatively straight up the hill. Eureka Peak can be seen through the trees to the east. The musical sound of the stream can be heard for the first part of the trail. Also listen for the liquid song of the thrush and the whirr of the mountain grouse. Wildflowers abound—bunchberries, anemones, columbine, wild strawberries, paintbrush, clintonia, lupine, penstemon, and Mt Hood lilies. The forest is pleasantly open with mixed conifers including Douglas fir, hemlock, white pine, lodgepole, and cedar.

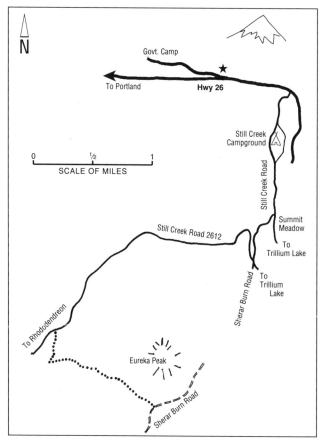

FROG BUTTE AND LOWER TWIN LAKE LOOP
Moderate (1,500 ft elevation gain)
6 mile loop, 3½–4½ hours
Map: USGS, Wapinitia Pass Quadrangle

Description: A moderately strenuous loop through beautiful and changing forest with a spectacular view of Mt Hood from the top of Frog Butte, and a chance to swim or fish in Lower Twin Lake. The trail climbs gently but steadily from Frog Lake to the top of Frog Butte, then drops steadily to Lower Twin Lake. The trails are all well-maintained, and easy to follow.

Access: From the Summit Rest Area at the far (east) end of the Government Camp business loop, go east on Hwy 26. At 2.2 miles, the road divides with Hwy 35 to Hood River taking off to the right and Hwy 26 continuing straight. Stay on Hwy 26 for another 6.9 miles and turn into a large parking area on the left side of the highway, signed to Frog Lake Campground. Follow Road #2610 from the parking area towards the campground to a fork at 0.4 miles. The right fork goes to the campground. Continue straight for another 0.2 miles to the trailhead on the left side of the road. Parking is available beside the road. The trail climbs steadily at an easy grade, crosses a clearcut and the forest road up to the Butte, and continues up (at a steeper grade) for 1½ miles to a T-junction. To climb to the top of the Butte, turn right (trail #530) and continue to climb for another ½ mile. When the trail reaches the clearcut at the top, turn right and find a rough road that winds round to the summit. To continue to Lower Twin Lake, return to the T-junction ½ mile below the summit clearcut and continue straight for 1½ miles until the trail reaches Lower Twin Lake. Continue counterclockwise round the lake to the camp sites at the north end. The trail takes off at the NE corner of the lake, climbs very briefly and joins the trail that goes to Upper Twin Lake. Turn left, signed to Wapanita Pass 2 miles, loop to the north of the lake and climb gradually back above the lake, over Twin Lake summit, and down to meet the Pacific Crest Trail

(#2000) at a T-junction. Take the left fork, signed to
Wapanita Pass, for 1½ miles to the large parking area.
Either take the trail just before the parking area, signed
Frog Lake ½ mile, or cross the parking area. Both will
lead to Road #2610 and back to your car.

Features: This lovely loop offers spectacular views of
Mt Hood, swimming, fishing, and beautiful, open forest
with plentiful huckleberries, moss-festooned trees, and
relatively unused trails as far as Lower Twin Lake.

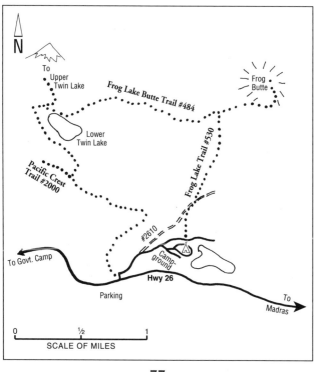

PIONEER WOMAN'S GRAVE
Easy (trail is flat but indistinct in places)
2 mile loop, 1 hour
Map: USGS, Mt Hood South Quadrangle

Description: A very easy, short, and interesting loop hike, suitable for all ages. The trail starts at the Pioneer Woman's Grave, crosses a clearcut and the East Fork of the Salmon River, follows a forest road, and winds through a beautiful segment of forest. This is a cross-country ski trail in winter, and not much used the rest of the year. A short section through the forest is not well marked and you need to be able to follow the blue, diamond-shaped ski trail markers high up on the trees. Don't take this trail if you only feel comfortable on the well-maintained and well-marked trails. You can't get lost, however, because Hwy 35 is close enough to hear some traffic noise in the section that goes through the forest.

Access: Take Hwy 26 east from Government Camp and when the road branches at 2.2 miles, take the right fork, Hwy 35, signed to Hood River. The road to the Pioneer Woman's Grave takes off to the right almost immediately, and is signed. The grave site is on the right, 0.4 miles from the highway. The hiking/skiing loop starts on the left of the road, behind the Forest Service sign. To find the trailhead, stand on the road facing the sign and look behind, and to the right of, the sign. The trail divides immediately after it enters the forest. Take the left fork, cross the log bridge over a stream, and follow the blue markers on poles that indicate the ski trail through the clearcut. The trail is quite indistinct here, so watch carefully for the markers. The trail joins a forest road; follow this to T-junction and take the right fork, over the East Fork of the Salmon River—only a stream at this point. Keep following the blue diamond-shaped ski trail markers along the forest road, watch for them to switch from the right to the left side of the road, and look for a black arrow on one of the markers indicating that the trail enters the forest on the left. This next section through the trees needs caution because it is not well-marked. Always have the next blue marker in sight before leaving the last. Follow the markers for about another ¾ mile until the trail joins the road to the Pioneer Woman's Grave. The parking place is a short distance to the left.

Features: The Pioneer Woman's Grave is worth a visit by itself because it brings the history of Oregon alive and evokes the hardships the pioneers must have endured on this difficult and challenging part of their trek. The hike is a delightful addition to the visit to the grave, and offers a spectacular view of Mt Hood (from the forest road), many flowers in the clearcut and beside the streams and road, and a chance to see deer. This is not a trail for the timid soul who likes to follow a well-beaten path; you do need to watch for the ski trail markers, but this adds to the sense of adventure.

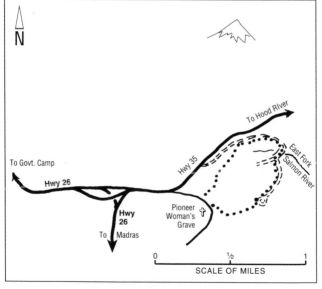

STILL CREEK TRAIL
Easy (good trail, very little elevation gain)
3.2 miles roundtrip, 2–3 hours
Map: USGS, Government Camp Quadrangle

Description: A delightful, short hike (#780), only 1.6 miles in each direction, with great views, shade, flowers, and a relatively open forest. There are only a few short sections where the grade is a little steep; the rest of the trail is flat or has very gentle grades, and is suitable for all ages and fitness levels.

Access: 1) *From the Summit Rest Area* at the far (east) end of the Government Camp business loop, go east on Hwy 26 and take the Mt Hood National Forest Still Creek Campground exit on the right (Road #2650), ½ mile from the Rest Area. The road loops through the campground— keep straight when it loops back—and continue to a large open meadow, Summit Meadow. N   ginning of the meadow, at a junction, take the   and continue to a 4-way intersection after ½   the first (sharp) right road, Still Creek R   ollow this for 7.4 miles on an unpaved road wit   otholes (suitable for a passenger car). The trail   hard to spot, so watch your odometer and lo   e entrance to a campground on the south   the road after you have crossed three bridges o   ill Creek. The trailhead is hidden in shrubs opposite the campground entrance. There is space for parking for a few cars at the side of the road. The trail climbs at first, then flattens out and goes gently downhill. It crosses an unpaved forest road, and a paved road, then dips down to the Zigzag River. To get to Camp Creek Campground, follow the trail to the left when it reaches the river and cross the bridge.

2) *From Portland:* Drive east on Hwy 26 to Rhododendron and at the far (east) end of the village turn southeast on Road #20 and continue for 1.1 miles to Still Creek Road #2612. Turn east and follow Still Creek Road for 3.5 miles. The trailhead is on the left of the road, about 0.1 mile after a bridge and opposite an unmarked campground entrance.

Features: A perfect walk for a day when you aren't feeling very energetic, but want to get out in the woods and the hills. Also a perfect hike for all members of the family and those out-of-town guests who want to see the countryside without the hoards that mob the Columbia Gorge. This is a very peaceful spot with many flowers in spring and summer, and majestic cathedral-like trees in some sections of the trail. The forest changes from young small trees with no undergrowth, to more mature forest with moss-covered logs, stumps and rocks, and rich undergrowth. There are great mushrooms in the fall.

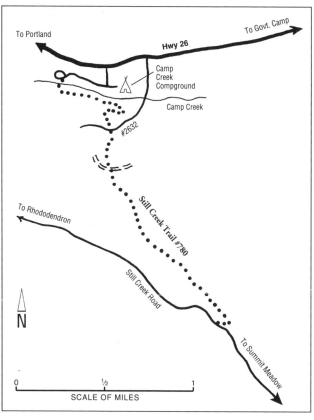

OLD SALMON RIVER TRAIL
Easy (flat, well-maintained trail)
2.4 miles one way with car shuttle, $1\frac{1}{4}$–$1\frac{1}{2}$ hours;
**   4.8 miles rountrip, $2\frac{1}{2}$–3 hours**
Map: USGS, Rhododendron Quadrangle

Description: A very accessible trail (#742A) along the
Salmon River through a cathedral-like forest with old
growth trees. The trail is excellent and, after the short
steep descent to the river, has virtually no elevation gain
or loss–so it is suitable for the whole family. The
roundtrip distance is 4.8 miles, or 2.4 miles one way
with an easy car shuttle.

Car shuttle: Leave one car at the bridge over the
Salmon River, about 2.4 miles from the trailhead, and the
other at the trailhead.

Access: The trailhead is on the Old Salmon River Road
off Hwy 26 at Wemme. *From Portland,* take Hwy 26
east towards Mt Hood. *From Government Camp,* take
Hwy 26 west towards Portland. At Wemme turn south at
the traffic light by the shopping centre onto Welches
Road (#2618), and continue on this road for 2.5 miles,
passing The Resort at the Mountain and keeping left at
the Y-junction at 2 miles, until you meet the Old Salmon
River Road. Turn right onto the Old Salmon River Road.
The trailhead is on the right, 0.7 miles past the junction,
and is marked by a sign "The Old Salmon River Trail" on
the left of the highway. There is usually ample parking
on the right, beside the trailhead. The trail dips down
immediately to the edge of the Salmon River, and follows it for the whole length, joining the road briefly for
two segments. The trail ends at a bridge over the Salmon
River, and continues on the east (left) side of the road as
the Salmon River Trail.

Features: This trail provides one of the most accessible opportunities to see the majesty of old growth trees. This is a mature forest so there are trees at all stages of growth—a superb place to see "nurse" logs overgrown with mosses, ferns, and ground cover, and sprouting shrubs and trees. The river provides an attraction equal to the forest, and is within sight for most of the trail. The sound of the river easily drowns out the traffic noise from the nearby road. This is a great spot to see salmon spawing in the fall (October).

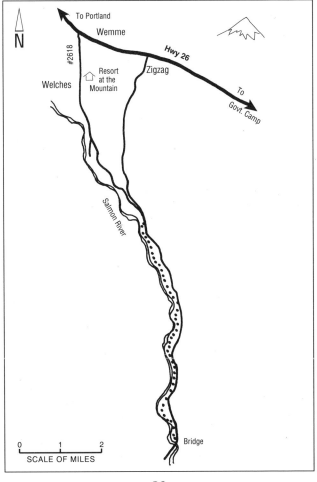

83

LOST CREEK NATURE TRAIL
Easiest
½ mile loop, ½ hour at leisurely pace
Map: USGS, Bull Run Quadrangle

Description: A delightful, flat, mostly paved trail through a beautiful grove of trees with interesting interpretive plaques that provide information about the area's flora, fauna, and geography. The trail was built by volunteers in 1972 to make an outdoor experience accessible to all. Benches are placed strategically and conveniently along the trail, as are wheelchair-accessible toilets. This is an ideal short, easy trail suitable for young children as well as those who are less mobile.

Access: The trailhead is 6.1 miles northeast of the Lolo Pass Road junction with Hwy 26 in Zigzag, 18 miles east of Sandy and 11.6 miles west of the Summit Rest Area at the far (east) end of the Government Camp business loop. From the junction, turn north on the Lolo Pass Road, drive 4.2 miles and turn right onto a paved road, signed Road #1825 to McNeil and Riley Campgrounds and Lost Creek Trail. Continue for 2.4 miles to a fork. Take the right fork (still Road #1825) signed to Lost Creek. The parking for the trail is 0.3 miles from the fork. The trail, shaped like a keyhole, is easy to follow and winds through the trees, round to viewpoints over the creek, and by beaver ponds. The short section that is unpaved has a broad, sturdy wooden boardwalk.

Features: The interpretive plaques explain how nature has formed this beautiful spot, in part from a mudflow from Mt Hood over 200 years ago. The majestic trees, lichens, lush mosses and ferns convey a special atmosphere. This is a lovely trail to introduce children to the beauty of the outdoors. They may particularly enjoy looking at the nurse logs—portions of fallen trees that are nurturing the growth of new plants and trees. The drive to the trailhead is also attractive with moss covering the rocks, banks, and forest floor. There is a very pleasant campground beside the trail.

Maidenhair Fern

N

McNeil
Campground   #1825

**Lost Creek
Nature Trail**

#1825

Lost Creek
Campground

#1825

Riley
Horse Camp

To
Portland

To Lolo Pass

Zigzag

Zigzag
Ranger Station

Hwy 26

To
Government Camp

NOT TO SCALE

FROM TIMBERLINE LODGE

Timberline Lodge provides easy access to the Timberline Trail (#600) that circles Mt Hood (40.7 miles), dipping in and out of a number of canyons, over streams and fair sized rivers, sometimes at the treeline, sometimes above or below it. The scenery is spectacular, and the summer wildflowers are glorious. Snow often remains on parts of the Timberline Trail well into July, and begins to fall again in October or November. A portion of the Pacific Crest Trail (#2000) lies along the section of Timberline Trail to the east and west of Timberline Lodge.

There are a number of attractive options for day hikes and walks from Timberline Lodge. These include hikes on Timberline Trail in a clockwise or counterclockwise direction, hikes down to Government Camp following winter ski trails, and hikes that combine parts of the Timberline Trail with trails that drop down to the Kiwanis Camp Road off Hwy 26 below Government Camp, or to the Mt. Hood Meadows Ski Resort on Hwy 35. Some of the hikes enter the Mt Hood Wilderness, where permits are required. The entrance is clearly marked by a sign and a registration box. All you need to do is sign in on the form provided in the box.

Timberline Lodge provides a convenient starting point for hikes. Parking is easy. The main Lodge and Wy'east Day Lodge offer a range of options for refreshments, plus a gift shop and ski rental area. Timberline Lodge is a remarkable and impressive building and well worth a visit. Built in the mid-1930s as a project of the Works Progress Administration, it has been lovingly maintained and restored by the US Forest Service, Friends of Timberline, and the RLK Corporation. It is a wonderful

Stunted Alpine Tree

place to stay or just to linger and enjoy the ambience. The handcrafted furnishings are perfectly suited to the Lodge and its setting, and the views in every direction are stunning. Function, art and whimsy combine to make the inside of the Lodge striking. The staircase newel posts are carved in the form of a variety of animals that invite you to touch and fondle them.

MOUNTAINEER LOOP AND SILCOX HUT
Strenuous (1,100 ft elevation gain)
2¾ mile loop, 2–3 hours
Map: USGS, Mt Hood South Quadrangle

Description: This trail (#798) starts and ends at
Timberline Lodge, and offers an attractive route up to
the Silcox Hut through an alpine flower garden. The
climb to the Silcox Hut is only 1,100 ft but is strenuous
because it is steep and starts at 6,000 ft.

Access: To reach Timberline Lodge from Government
Camp, take Hwy 26 east from the Summit Rest Area at
the far (east) end of the Government Camp business
loop, turn left (north) on to Timberline Road and drive
5.2 miles to the parking areas for Timberline Lodge.
Walk west past the Lodge on the paved service road that
leads to the chairlifts. The Mountaineer Trail (#798)
starts just beyond the Magic Mile Chairlift, about 200
yards from the Lodge. The trail marker can be seen easily
from the service road as it divides at a Y-junction. The
trail meanders through the trees and alpine meadows
and meets and crosses the Timberline Trail after ½ mile.
Continue on the Mountaineer Trail to the top of
the Magic Mile Chairlift. The trail is well marked at first
but becomes indistinct towards the top. Since the top of
the chairlift is always in sight, finding your way is not a
problem. From the top of the chairlift, make your way
over to the Silcox Hut, about 300 yards to the east.
Return to Timberline Lodge on the service road from the
Silcox Hut, now a Forest Service Interpretive Trail.

Features: The spectacular views and alpine flowers
makes this a glorious hike. The Silcox Hut was built in
1939 as the warming hut and upper motor house for the
original Magic Mile Chairlift. Recently renovated, thanks
to many volunteers, it is again open for food and lodging. The Forest Service Interpretive Trail is a self-guided
walk from the top of the chairlift to Timberline Lodge.
Numbered posts along the way correspond to information in a Forest Service pamphlet (available at the lodge)
about the way the altitude and weather shape the land-

scape and plants, and which animals can survive in this challenging environment.

Alternative: The Magic Mile Chairlift offers an easy way to get to the Silcox Hut and walk down the Forest Service Interpretive Trail. Foot passengers can use the lift in the summer. The 1994 summer rates were $6 for adults, $3 for children 7-12 years, $15 for families.

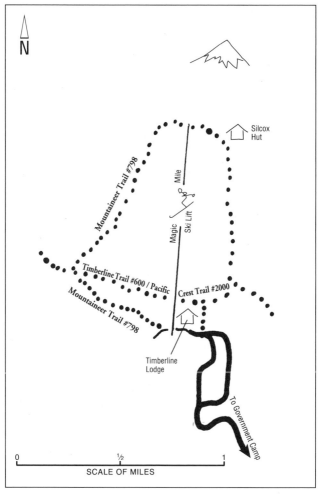

PARADISE PARK LOOP
Strenuous (2,300 ft elevation gain)
9.6 miles roundtrip, 5–6 hours; 12.2 full loop, 6–7 hours
Map: USGS, Mt Hood South Quadrangle

Description: One of the most spectacular hikes on Mt Hood, especially when the alpine flowers are in bloom in June, July, and August. The trail (#757) dips in and out of several sizable canyons, mostly in the trees just below the timberline. The views north to Mt Hood, and south to Mt Jefferson are truly sensational. Most of this hike is on the Timberline Trail (#600) that circles Mt Hood, so it is very well-maintained and well-graded. It is quite strenuous, however, since it involves about a 2,300 ft elevation gain at 6,000 ft altitude. The trail may be dusty in late August if the summer is very dry. Since part of this hike is in the Mt Hood Wilderness, be sure to sign in at the registration box about 1½ miles from Timberline Lodge.

Access: From the Summit Rest Area at the far (east) end of the Government Camp business loop, take Hwy 26 east for ¼ mile, turn left onto Timberline Road, and drive 5.2 miles to the parking areas for Timberline Lodge. Walk past the Lodge on the paved service road that leads to the chairlifts. The trail starts as the Mountaineer Trail (#798), just above the lower end of the Magic Mile Chairlift, about 200 yards west of the Lodge. The trail marker can be seen easily from the service road as it divides at a Y-junction. The trail winds in and out of the trees and joins the Timberline Trail (#600) after about ½ mile where the foundation of the old Timberline Cabin can still be seen on the left. Continue on the trail, now the Timberline Trail, passing the trail to Hidden Lake at 1½ miles from Timberline Lodge, and dipping in and out of two small canyons (Sand and Little Zigzag) and one deep canyon (Zigzag). The trail drops 750 ft into Zigzag Canyon, crosses the stream that is the headwaters of the Zigzag River, and climbs 980 ft to the western rim. About ¼ mile from the bottom of the canyon, before you reach the top, the trail divides. Take the right fork, Paradise Park Loop Trail, to climb up to Paradise Park; the left is the continuation of the Timberline Trail. Paradise Park is the open meadow area above the timberline, about one mile from the fork. The Paradise Park Loop Trail intersects with the Paradise Park Trail (#778) in the meadow. Return the same way, or take the Paradise Park Trail to the left and rejoin the Timberline Trail, turning left again when you join the Timberline Trail; or continue on and complete the Paradise Park Loop, rejoining the Timberline Trail after 2.4 miles, and turning left (east) onto the trail that brings you back to Timberline Lodge.

Features: As if the magnificent views were not enough, the trail is rich with alpine meadows and flowers: beargrass, paintbrush, lupine, penstemon, and avalanche lilies flourish in the meadows, and yellow and pink monkey flowers cluster by the streams. Zigzag Canyon is an impressive gash on the flank of the mountain and a reminder of the forces that shape the mountains.

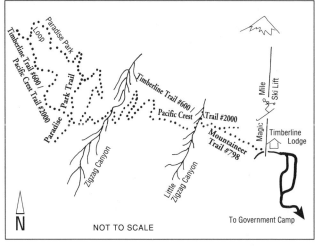

TIMBERLINE AND PARADISE PARK TRAILS
Strenuous (long hike, some uphill, mostly downhill)
9.2 miles one way, 5–6 hours
Maps: Mt Hood South & Government Camp
   Quadrangles

Description: A long, but beautiful hike that starts at
Timberline Lodge, follows the Timberline Trail (#600)
for 4 miles, then drops steadily for almost 2,500 ft over
5.2 miles to the Kiwanis Camp Road off Hwy 26, below
Government Camp. As described, the hike requires a car
shuttle. The Timberline Trail portion dips in and out of
several canyons, is mostly in the trees just below the timberline, and is well-travelled and well-maintained. The
Paradise Park Trail portion is through beautiful, varied
forest with abundant rhododendrons in the lower
stretches. This portion is much less travelled but the trail
is well-maintained and the grade mostly quite gentle.
Since part of this hike is in the Mt Hood Wilderness, be
sure to sign in at the registration box and 1½ miles from
Timberline Lodge.

Car Shuttle: Leave one car at the trailhead in the camp-
ground on the left (west) side of the Kiwanis Camp
Road, 1.2 miles from its junction with Hwy 26. The
Kiwanis Camp Road (#39) is 5 miles west of
Government Camp on Hwy 26 between mileposts 48
and 49, and 4.1miles east of Rhododendron. Park the
other car at Timberline Lodge, 5.2 miles northeast of
Government Camp on the Timberline Road off Hwy 26.

Access: Walk west past Timberline Lodge on the paved
service road that leads to the chairlifts. The trail starts as
the Mountaineer Trail (#798), just beyond the Magic
Mile chairlift, about 200 yards west of the Lodge. The
trail marker can be seen easily from the service road as it
divides at a Y-junction. The trail winds in and out of the
trees and joins the Timberline Trail (#600) after about ½
mile. Continue left (west) on the trail, passing the trail to
Hidden Lake at 1½ miles from the Lodge, and dipping in
and out of two small canyons (Sand and Little Zigzag)
and one deep canyon (Zigzag). There is a 750 ft eleva-

tion loss into Zigzag Canyon and a 980 ft climb to its western rim. About ¼ mile from the river, the trail divides: the right fork climbs to Paradise Park—a spectacular open area above the treeline; Timberline Trail continues straight ahead (signed Pacific Crest Trail). Both options are interesting. Paradise Park requires an additional climb, but is well worth the effort if you have the time and energy. If you are continuing straight on

Continued on page 94

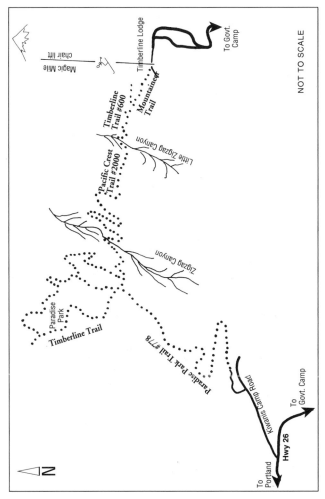

Timberline Trail, turn left onto the Paradise Park Trail
(#778) about ¼ mile after the fork, and follow it down
for 5.2 miles to the trailhead on the Kiwanis Camp Road.
If you detour up to Paradise Park, take the Paradise Park
Trail (#778) to the left at the trail intersection in the
meadow.

Features: The views on the Timberline Trail portion of
this hike are spectacular. Mt Hood dominates the view
to the north, and to the south, Mt Jefferson, Three
Sisters, and the forested land in between provide an end-
less vista of rugged and largely uninhabited country. This
is a perfect hike for the flower-lover: alpine flowers
abound on Timberline Trail once the snow has melted;
banks of rhododendrons crowd the edge of Paradise
Park Trail, and are in full bloom in early summer. The
forest is constantly changing in character and interest.

Rhododendron

MOUNTAINEER–TIMBERLINE LOOP

Easy
1½ mile, ¾–1 hour
Map: USGS, Mt Hood South Quadrangle

Description: A beautiful, short loop from Timberline Lodge through alpine meadows and stunted trees.

Access: This gentle walk starts and ends at Timberline Lodge. To reach the Lodge from Government Camp, take Hwy 26 east from the Summit Rest Area at the far (east) end of the Government Camp business loop, turn left (north) onto Timberline Road and drive 5.2 miles to the parking areas for Timberline Lodge. Walk west past the Lodge on the paved service road that leads to the chairlifts. The trail starts as the Mountaineer Trail (#798), just beyond the Magic Mile Chairlift, about 200 yards west of the Lodge. The trail meanders through the trees and alpine meadows and joins the Timberline Trail after about ½ mile. Turn right onto Timberline Trail (#600) to return to the Lodge, about ¾ mile.

Features: An easy walk, just below the timberline. The views are spectacular: Mt Hood looms to the north and Mt Jefferson, Three Sisters, Trillium Lake, and the Salmon-Huckleberry Wilderness spread out to the south. The alpine flowers are so prolific in the summer that it feels like walking through an alpine garden.

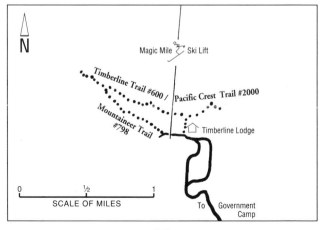

DEADMAN'S CURVE TRAIL
Easy
2.0 mile roundtrip, 1½ hours
Map: USGS, Government Camp Quadrangle

Description: A gentle walk along an old logging road through an old growth forest that has been selectively cut. Several short spur trails on the right overlook the Salmon River Canyon.

Access: 1) *From the Summit Rest Area* at the far (east) end of the Government Camp business loop: Drive east on Hwy 26 ¼ mile and turn left (north) on to Timberline Road. The trailhead is on the upper (northern) side of a wide hairpin turn on the Timberline Road about 2.9 miles from Hwy 26. Park on the downhill side of the highway, just above the curve. The trail starts just beyond the guardrail as an overgrown road, loops back and above the highway, then veers away from the highway for a while and meanders through the open forest. There are several short logging spurs to the right that are worth exploring. The road climbs gradually and joins the Timberline road after about a mile. Return the same way.

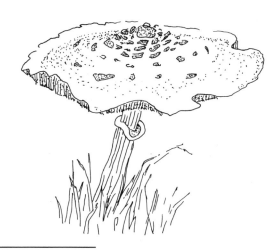

Amanita Mushroom

2) *From Timberline Lodge:* Drive down Timberline Road towards Government Camp for about 2.3 miles and park on the right of the road, just before a 90° righthand bend. Then follow the same instructions as above.

Features: This woodland road makes for a friendly walk, as walkers may go side by side rather than single file. There are open glades with beargrass, forage for deer and abundant huckleberries in August.

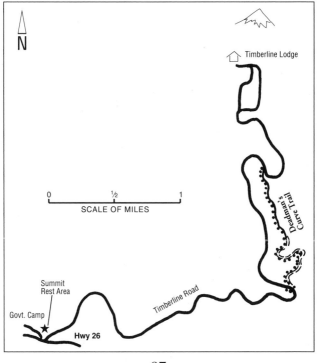

TIMBERLINE–UMBRELLA TRAIL
Moderately strenuous; requires a river crossing
6 miles one way with car shuttle, 3–4 hours
Map: USGS, Mt Hood South Quadrangle

Description: A gorgeous trail that showcases alpine meadows and flowers. This hike works well as a one-way trail with a car shuttle, or as a roundtrip. The trail dips into White River Canyon and climbs out again.

Car Shuttle: Leave one car at the Umbrella Falls trailhead 1.5 miles up on the access road to Mt Hood Meadows Ski area, 8.9 miles east of Government Camp on Hwy 35. To reach the Mt Hood Meadows road, take Hwy 26 east of Government Camp. At the first major junction, take the Hood River exit which is Hwy 35. The Mt Hood Meadows access road is 6.8 miles from this junction, on the left. Leave the other car at Timberline Lodge.

Access: From the Summit Rest Area at the far (east) end of the Government Camp business loop, take Hwy 26 east for about ¼ mile, turn left onto Timberline Road, and drive 5.2 miles to the Timberline Lodge parking areas. Park in the unpaved lower lot on the north side of Timberline Road (the first one on the right), and look for a trail that climbs up the bank at the far end of the parking lot. The trail heads up the mountain, veers slightly to the right and soon descends into a shallow gully. You are now on the Timberline Trail (#600) that circles Mt Hood. Continue on this well-marked trail, ignoring a fork that leads to a viewpoint, and continuing to the next fork 1½ miles from Timberline Lodge where the Timberline Trail takes off to the left and the Pacific Crest Trail (#2000) continues straight, signed to Barlow Pass. Take the Timberline Trail to the left, and stay on it as it crosses the White River Canyon, and climbs out the other side. The trail is well marked by stone cairns and posts as it crosses the wide canyon bed. Crossing the White River is sporting and needs care, so look for a suitable crossing place. The trail that climbs out of the canyon starts in the draw of trees that dips down to the edge of the canyon, zigzags up for about a mile, then flattens out at the treeline and continues through alpine meadows. Four miles east of Timberline Lodge, the trail crosses a service road leading to Mt Hood Meadows Ski area. Just before the service road, the trail forks. Take the fork that bends sharply to the right, signed the Umbrella Falls Trail, and follow it for 1½ miles to the Mt Hood Meadows access road. Umbrella Falls is ¼ mile the other side of the access road on the continuation of the Umbrella Falls Trail.

Features: This hike is hard to top: the views of Mt Hood are breathaking, the alpine flowers and meadows are gorgeous, and the vistas south, once you're out of White River Canyon, are spectacular. The broad swath of the canyon is a reminder of the awesome power of Mother Nature. The images of this hike will stay with you for a long time.

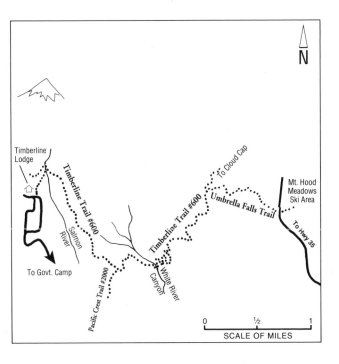

TIMBERLINE–YELLOWJACKET TRAIL
Strenuous (mostly downhill but rough going and hard-to-follow trail)
10½ miles one way with car shuttle, 5½–6½ hours
Map: USGS, Mt Hood South Quadrangle

Description: A challenging, exhilarating, adventurous hike that descends 2,500 ft from Timberline Lodge to Government Camp 3½ miles on the Pacific Crest Trail, and 7 miles on Yellowjacket Trail—a cross-country ski trail that was not built for hiking, nor maintained. The challenge and adventure come from the need to follow the ski trail markers on Yellowjacket Trail through numerous swampy areas, knee- to waist-high bushes and grasses, and across streams. THIS IS NOT A HIKE TO DO ALONE!! Sturdy boots are recomended and take your 10 essentials! Also take care to minimize the impact on the fragile wet areas.

Car Shuttle: Leave one car at the Summit Rest Area at the far (east) end of the Government Camp business loop, and the other at Timberline Lodge.

Access: This hike starts above and east of Timberline Lodge. To reach Timberline Lodge, turn left onto Timberline Road from Hwy 26, ¼ east of the Summit Rest area at the far (east) end of the Government Camp business loop. Drive 5.2 miles up to the lower unpaved Timberline Lodge parking lot on the north side of Timberline Road (the first one on the right), and look for a trail that climbs up the bank at the far end of the lot. The trail soon veers slightly to the right and descends into a shallow canyon. You are now on the Timberline Trail #600. Continue straight at the first fork, ignoring the left spur that goes to a viewpoint. The next fork is a crucial one: the left fork is the Timberline Trail; straight ahead is the Pacific Crest Trail (#2000). Follow the Pacific Crest Trail for another 2 miles, going steadily downhill, to the intersection with Yellowjacket Trail, which is marked by blue diamond-shaped ski trail markers high on the trees. The intesection is NOT obvious; look for a blue arrow pointing to the right at the first tree with the blue markers. If you reach a tree with a trail sign, you have gone too for, so retrace your steps for ¼ mile. From this point on, the secret is to make sure you can ALWAYS see the next blue marker before you lose sight of the last one. For the first ½ mile, the going is quite rough—through swampy areas and shrubs and over trees and branches. Arrows on the ski signs show where the trail changes direction. The trail becomes easier after a while, dips into and out of Salmon River Canyon, and follows close to the edge of the canyon. Many log bridges, swampy areas, and stream crossings lie ahead, but hang in there—it's worth the effort. When the trail meets a service road, turn right and when you intersect with another service road, turn right again and follow this road for about ¼ mile until you reach another service road on the left (#149). Turn left and immediately look for a brown ski trail sign and blue trail markers high on the trees up the bank as the road bends to the left. As before, follow the blue markers carefully. This section of the Yellowjacket Trail is better marked and less sporting than the eastern portion, but still needs care, especially through the logged area. At one point, the trail joins a service road to Snowbunny Lodge. Go right here for about 100 yards and find the continuation

Continued on page 102

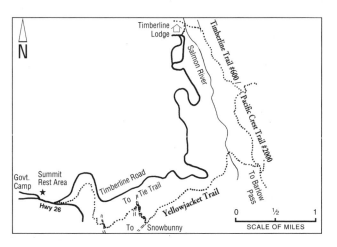

of the trail on the left of the road. The trail meets the Timberline Road just above its intersection with Hwy 26. The Summit Rest Area is ¼ mile to the right (west) on Hwy 26.

Features: This spectacular hike starts with beautiful alpine meadows, and majestic views of Mt Hood, then descends into quiet forest before setting out on an adventurous cross-country bushwhack. The frequent swampy areas and streams contrast strikingly with the drier, more austere forest and provide a habitat for wetland flowers. Look for animal tracks, especially in the muddy areas. Huckleberries are plentiful in August.

Beargrass

TIMBERLINE AND HIDDEN LAKE TRAILS
Moderate
6 miles one way; car shuttle needed
Maps: USGS, Mt. Hood South Quadrangle

Description: A 6-mile hike (one way) from Timberline Lodge to the Kiwanis Camp Road near Hwy 26, west and below Government Camp; 1½ miles with modest elevation gain on the Timberline Trail and 4½ miles steadily downhill on the Hidden Lake Trail #779. The Timberline trail portion is part through open forest with small trees, and part across ski runs. The downhill portion is through forest that varies in the size and density of the trees. A car shuttle is needed if this is to be a one-way hike.

Car shuttle: Leave one car at the trailhead on the left (west) side of the Kiwanis Camp Rd, 2.1 miles from its junction with Hwy 26. The Kiwanis Camp Rd is 5.1 miles west of the Summit Rest Area at the east end of Government Camp. Leave the other car at Timberline Lodge.

Access: From the Summit Rest Area at the far (east) end of the Government Camp business loop, take Hwy 26 east ¼ mile, turn left onto Timberline Rd, and drive 5.2 miles to the parking area for Timberline Lodge. Walk past the Lodge on the paved road that leads to the chairlifts. The trail starts as the Mountaineer Trail (#798), just past the bottom end of the Magic Mile chairlift, about 200 yards west of Timberline Lodge. The trail marker can be seen easily from the service road as it divides at a Y-junction. The trail wends in and out of the trees and joins the Timberline Trail at the ruins of an old cabin. Continue on the trail for 1½ miles, past the wilderness permit box (remember to sign in) to a well-marked junction with the Hidden Lake Trail (#779). Turn left onto the Hidden Lake Trail and follow this, going downhill steadily for 2 miles to a T-junction. Hidden Lake is 50 yards on the left fork. The main trail goes to the right and crosses the outflow stream from the lake. The trailhead is another 2 miles beyond the lake.

Features: The early portion of the hike has spectacular views of Mt Hood to the north and Mt Jefferson to the south. The flowers on the two portions of the hike are quite different: phlox, partidge foot, alpine lupine, paintbrush and cat's ear lilies are plentiful on the Timberline Trail portion. Once into the forest, the flowers are mainly white: bunchberry, foam flower, avalanche lily, and clintonia are abundant beside the trail, and banks of rhododendrons which bloom in June/July line much of the trail. Listen for the liquid note of the hermit thrush. Hidden Lake is weedy and shallow and not suitable for swimming or fishing.

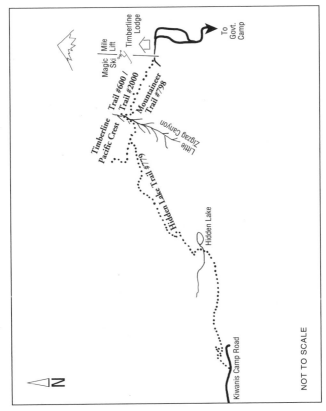

BURIED FOREST OVERLOOK
Easy
1.2 miles roundtrip, 1 hour
Map: USGS, Mt Hood South Quadrangle

Description: An easy walk on a portion of the Timberline Trail (#600) that circles Mt Hood. The goal of the walk is the overlook into the White River Canyon and the forest that was buried in the canyon when Mt Hood last erupted over 200 years ago. The overlook is not fenced, so take care—a bit scary for those who do not have a head for heights!

Access: This walk starts and ends at Timberline Lodge. To reach Timberline Lodge from Government Camp, take Hwy 26 east from the Summit Rest Area at the far (east) end of the Government Camp business loop, turn left (north) onto Timberline Road, and drive 5.2 miles to the Timberline Lodge parking areas. Park at the lower unpaved lot on the north side of Timberline Road (the first one you see on the right) and look carefully for a trail that climbs up the bank at the far end of the lot. Follow the trail as it veers slightly to the right and descends into a shallow canyon. You are now on the Timberline Trail #600 and the Pacific Crest Trail #2000. At the first fork, take the left trail marked Buried Forest, and continue to the viewpoint. To return, retrace your steps.

Features: The spectacular views of Mt Hood to the north and Mt Jefferson, the Three Sisters and the Salmon-Huckleberry Wilderness to the south, glorious alpine meadows, weirdly-shaped snags and imposing glacial morraines make this a walk you will remember for a long time. Look for paintbrush, penstemon, yarrow, beargrass, cat's ear lilies, partridge foot, pussy paws, and lupine.

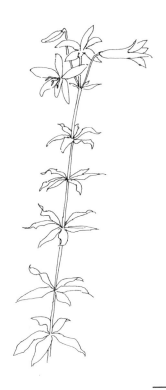

Mt. Hood Lily

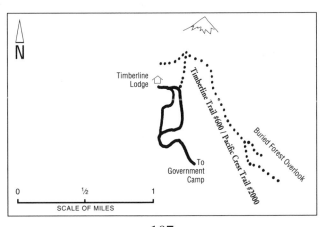

ALPINE TRAIL TO GOVERNMENT CAMP
Moderate (2,100 ft elevation drop)
**3 miles one way, 1½–2 hours; 6 miles roundtrip,
   3½–4½ hours**
Map: USGS, Government Camp Quadrangle

Description: This is one of the old service roads that
connect Timberline Lodge and Government Camp. It
serves as a ski trail in the winter and as a hiking and
mountain biking trail in summer. Most of the trail is
moderately steep. This trail is seldom used, so is very
peaceful. This hike works well as a one-way hike with
car shuttle, or as a vigorous roundtrip.

Car shuttle: Leave one car at the Summit Rest Area at
the far (east) end of the Government Camp business
loop and the other at Timberline Lodge.

Access: Alpine Trail starts just below the bottom of
Blossom Chairlift, 1 mile (by the **old** road—West Leg
Road) below Timberline Lodge. To reach Timberline
Lodge from the Summit Rest Area at the far (east) end of
the Government Camp business loop, take Hwy 26 east
for ¼ mile, turn left onto the Timberline Road and drive
5.2 miles to the Timberline Lodge parking areas. Walk
west past the Lodge on the paved service road that leads
to the chairlifts and continue on the service road as it
turns downhill after the Magic Mile chairlift. The rough
service road descends quite steeply for about 500 ft and
forks. Take the left fork that goes to the bottom of
Blossom Chairlift, and find the beginning of Alpine Trail
just below and to the right of the bottom of the chairlift.
The trail is not signed, but is obvious. The trail drops
steadily and comes out at the top of Summit Ski Area.
Summit Rest Area is at the bottom of the Ski Area.

Features: Alpine Trail is quite secluded and peaceful
and in early summer often has a glorious display of beargrass—as well as many other flowers. Listen for the
whirr of the mountain grouse, and watch for deer. Great
views south towards Mt Jefferson, Three Sisters, and
Trillium Lake.

Chanterelle

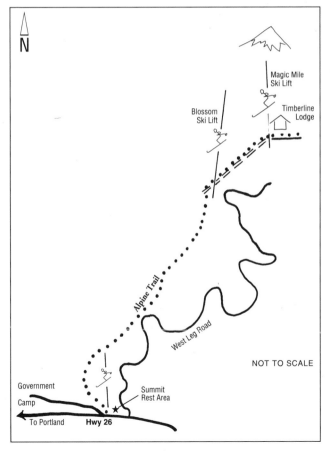

GLADE TRAIL TO GOVERNMENT CAMP

Moderate (2,100 ft elevation loss on service roads and trails)

3 miles one way, 1½–2 hours; 6 miles roundtrip, 3½–4½ hours

Maps: USGS, Mt Hood South and Government Camp Quadrangles

Description: A fairly easy one-way hike, and strenuous roundtrip, on service roads and trails that connect Timberline Lodge and Government Camp. These are downhill and cross-country trails in the winter and mountain bikes routes in the summer. Great views and abundant flowers.

Car Shuttle: Leave one car in Government Camp, or at the Summit Rest Area at the far (east) end of the Government Camp business loop, and the other at Timberline Lodge.

Access: This trail starts from Timberline Lodge. To reach the Lodge from Government Camp, take Hwy 26 east and turn left (north) on to Timberline Road ¼ mile east of the Summit Rest Area at the far (east) end of the Government Camp business loop. Timberline Lodge is 5.2 miles northeast of Hwy 26, and has ample parking. Walk west past the lodge on the paved service road that leads to the chairlifts and continue on the service road as it turns downhill after the Magic Mile Chairlift. The rough service road descends quite steeply for about 500 ft, then forks. Ignore the left fork that leads to the bottom of Blossom Chairlift, and continue downhill to a T-junction where there is a large orange sign for Glade Trail to the right. Take the right fork and follow this to Government Camp, ignoring the service roads that intersect with the trail. The only difficult intersection is just above the village where the trail turns left under a power line, just after a post that says Emergency Telephone. A service road continues straight. Glade Trail meets a paved road in the village. Follow this down to the main road. If your car is parked at the Summit Rest Area, turn left along the business loop for about ½ mile.

Features: This hike provides a satisfying workout (if hiked both ways) with fantastic views along the way. Flowers are plentiful, especially in early summer, and mushrooms abound lower down, in the fall. Listen for the whirr of the mountain grouse, and keep an eye out for deer.

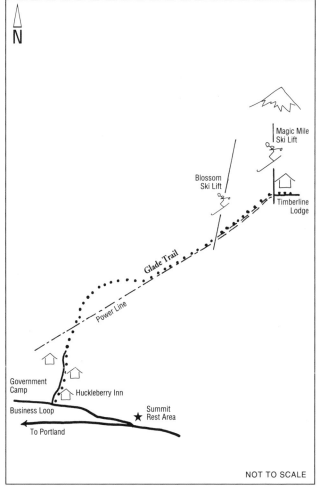

GLADE–ALPINE TRAIL LOOP
TO GOVERNMENT CAMP
Strenuous (2100ft elevation loss and gain)
6 mile loop, 3½- 4½ hours
Map: Mt Hood South Quadrangle

Description: A scenic loop on downhill and cross - country ski trails that connect Timberline Lodge and Government Camp.

Access: This loop starts from Timberline Lodge. To reach the Lodge from Government Camp, take Hwy26 east and turn left (north) onto the Timberline Road ¼ mile east of the Summit Rest Area at the far (east) end of the Government Camp business loop. Timberline Lodge is 5.2 miles northeast of Hwy 26, and has ample parking. Walk past the main Lodge on the paved service road that leads west to the chairlifts. The service road continues, now unpaved, and forks: take the left fork, heading downhill. The service road is initially steep and rough, but becomes easier after the about ¼ mile. Follow the road until you reach a Y-junction and see a large orange sign for Glade Trail to the right. Follow this to the right down to Government Camp, ignoring the service roads that intersect with the trail. The only difficult intersection is just above the village where the trail turns left under a power line, just after a post that says Emergency Telephone. A service road continues straight. Glade trail meets a paved road in the village. Follow this down to the main street, turn left and walk ½ mile on the business loop to the Summit Ski Area at the far (east) end of the business loop. To complete the loop, walk up the service road on the left side of the Summit Ski Area, behind the Day Lodge, to the top of the chairlift. Continue on the forest road to the left of the chairlift– now Alpine Trail–for about 2 miles to the bottom of Blossom Chairlift. The trail is actually an old rutted service road, rather than a trail, and is quite steep in sections; the steepest part is Big Mazama Hill. From the bottom of Blossom Chair, continue up the service road under the chairlift and turn right up the hill when you reach the wide ski run. This is the steep, rocky service road you started on and leads up to the Magic Mile Skilift and Timberline Lodge.

Features: A strenuous, beautiful hike with spectacular views north to Mt Hood and south to Mt Jefferson. Alpine Trail often has a spectacular display of beargrass in early summer–as well as many flowers. Listen for the whirr of the mountain grouse, and watch for deer and elk.

Alternative: A recently-built trail, Crosstown Trail #755, that loops around to the top of Government Camp, offers an attractive alternative way to complete this loop. The trail crosses Glade Trail just below the inter-section of the powerline and Glade Trail (see map). Turn left (east) onto the new trail and follow it to Summit Ski Area. Turn left and follow the instructions above.

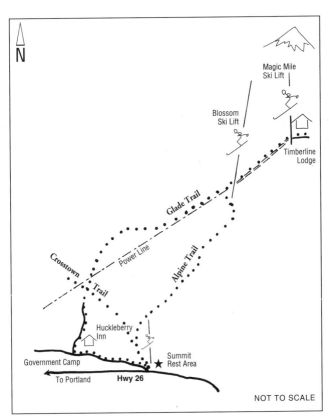

AREA CAMPGROUNDS

Alpine: Situated one mile from Timberline Lodge on Timberline Road so may not be snow free until late summer. 16 campsites, water, garbage, vault toilets. $7

Camp Creek: Located in a forested setting near Camp Creek. Access: 3 miles east of Rhododendron on Hwy 26; turn south to the campground. 18 single sites, 6 double sites, water, vault toilets, picnic sites, garbage. $8 single sites, $10 creekside/premiun single sites, $12 double sites, $3 additional vehicles.

Green Canyon: Located in an old growth forest, adjacent to the Salmon River. Access: At Zigzag, turn south on Salmon River Road (#2618) for 4 miles. 15 free campsites, 7 picnic sites, amphitheater, garbage, vault toilets, accessible toilet, some oversized trailer spaces. NO drinking water.

Lost Creek: The newest campground in the Zigzag Ranger District is barrier free. Access: At Zigzag turn north on Lolo Pass Road (# 18), and east on Rd #1825 after 4 miles. Follow signs to campground. 9 campsites, 5 pack-in sites, 2 group sites, picnic area. Fishing pier, nature trail, garbage, water, accessible toilets. $ 8 single sit, $16 group site, $3 additional vehicles.

McNeil: Situated in the Old Maid Flat area with views of Mt Hood. Access: At Zigzag turn north on Lolo Pass Road (#18), and east on Road # 1825 after 4 miles. 34 free campsites, garbage, vault toilets, NO drinking water.

Riley: A popular horse camp with access to several trail systems. Access: At Zigzag turn north on Lolo Pass Road (#18) and east on Road # 1825 after 4 miles and right on Road #380. 14 campsites, hitching posts, loading and staging area for horses, water, garbage, vault toilets. $8 single site, $3 additional vehicles.

Still Creek: Forested setting near Government Camp. Access: Turn south onto Still Creek Campground Road, 1/2 mile east of Government Camp. 27 campsites, water, vault toilets, garbage. $8 single site, $3 additional vehicles.

Tollgate: Located near the historic Barlow Road and Tollgate. Access: 1 mile east of Rhododendron on Hwy 26, turn south into the campground. 15 campsites, picnic sites, water, vault toilets, garbage. $8 single sites, $10 creekside/ premium, $3 additional vehicles.

Trillium: Located on Trillium Lake with views of Mt Hood. Access: From Hwy 26 turn south onto Road 2656 and follow signs to the campground. 55 campsites, picnic area, boat ramp, space for some oversized trailers, water, garbage, accessible toilet and vault toilets, fishing pier. $9 single site, $18 multiple family site, $11 lakeside/ premium single site, $3 additional vehicles.

Near Pioneer Woman's Grave

BUSINESS RESOURCES

Mt. Hood Visitors Information Center   503 622-4822
65000 E. Highway 26 (PO Box 342)
Welches OR 97067
Mt. Hood Recreation/Chamber of Commerce/Zigzag Ranger
District (USFS) partnership. "One-stop Information Center."

RESTAURANTS AND ACCOMODATIONS
Alpine Hut Restaurant   503 622-4618
73365 E. Hwy 26 (PO Box 263)
Rhododendron OR 97049
Breakfast, lunch, dinner and cocktails served in a unique mountain atmosphere; 7am-10pm

Barlow Trail Inn   503 622-3112
69580 E. Hwy 26 (PO Box 336, Welches, 97067)
Zigzag OR 97049
Breakfast, lunch, dinner, full lounge, large covered deck, air conditioned. Historic log building. Open 6:45am

The Brightwood Guest House B & B   503 622-5783
64725 E. Barlow Trail Road (PO Box 330)
Brightwood OR 97011

Cascade Property Management   503 622-5688
24403 E. Welches Rd., Suite 105D (PO Box 454)
Welches OR 97067
Cozy cabins, cottages, homes and contemporary condos close to skiing, hiking, golfing, biking and fishing. All homes are fully furnished. 10am-5pm Mon.-Sat., 12pm-5pm Sun.

Cedar Grove Cottage   503 557-8292
23782 E. Sampson Ave. (28350 SW Mtn Rd, West Linn, 97068)
Welches OR 97067
A romantic getaway located on a secluded acre of forested grounds in Welches. Kitchen, fireplace, spa.

Chalet Swiss Specialty Restaurant   503 622-3600
Hwy. 26 at Welches Rd. (PO Box 1222)
Welches OR 97067
A Mt. Hood dining tradition for 22 years. Featuring Swiss and Northwest Cuisine in a rustic alpine atmosphere. 5pm Wed.-Sun.

Charlie's Mountain View   503 272-3333
88462 Government Camp Loop (PO Box 10)
Government Camp OR 97028
Full service restaurant. Live music or karaoke. 11:30am-2:30am

Courtyard Cafe & Catering   503 622-5222
65000 E. Hwy 26, Mt Hood Village, Brightwood (PO Box 931,Welches,97067)
Brightwood OR 97011
First stop on the way to Mt. Hood from Portland. Breakfast, lunch, espresso,vegetarian specials, homemade pastries.
Catering and banquets. 7am-3pm

Don Guidos Italian Cuisine   503 622-5141
73330 E. Hwy. 26 (PO Box 365)
Rhododendron OR 97067
In the historic Log Lodge at the base of Mt. Hood. Open 5pm.

Falcon's Crest Inn   503 272-3403
87287 Government Camp Loop (PO Box 185)
Government Camp OR 97028
Lodging, bed & breakfast, dining, conference center, private
and mystery parties in Government Camp. Small groups welcome. Christmas holiday specialists. 6am–11pm daily

Fernwood at Alder Creek   503 622-3570
54850 E. Hwy 26
Sandy OR 97055
Bed and breakfast in a comfortable old log home overlooking a
rushing mountain stream. Private whirlpool tubs.

Golden Poles Chalet   503 272-3337
(PO Box 399)
Government Camp OR 97028
Condominiums. 8am–10pm daily

Honey Bear Express   503 622-5726
Hwy 26 & Welches Rd. (PO Box 1089)
Welches OR 97067
Deli sandwiches, daily specials and excellent soups.Espresso,
ice cream and candy. Take-out. 9am–5pm daily

Huckleberry Inn   503 272-3325
Government Camp Loop (PO Box 249)
Government Camp OR 97028
24 hours daily.

Michaels Bread & Breakfast   503 622-5333
24525 E. Welches Road (PO Box 367)
Welches OR 97067
Restaurant and bakery. 7 days, 7am–2pm

Mt. Hood Brew Pub   503 272-3724
87304 E. Government Camp Loop (c/o Timberline Lodge,
Timberline, OR 97028)
Government Camp OR 97028
Fresh ales and stout from Mt. Hood Brewing Co. Pizzas, sand-
wiches, salads, espresso and Starbuck's coffee. Noon -10pm
Sun.-Thurs., noon–11pm Fri. & Sat.

Mt. Hood Manor   503 272-3440
88900 Government Camp Loop (PO Box 369)
Government Camp OR 97028
Four spacious rooms, each with private bath, family-style
breakfast. TV/VCRs. Outdoor hot tub. Open year round.

Mt. Hood Village   503 253-9445
(65000 E. Highway 26)
Welches OR 97067
A five-star camping resort & Cafe. 24-hour security, indoor
pool, spa, saunas, fitness center, gas station and store/gift shop.

Old Welches Inn Bed & Breakfast　　　503 622-3754
26401 E Welches Road
Welches OR 97067
Bed & breakfast in the oldest establishment on the mountain.
The soothing sounds with the Salmon River in the back yard.
10am–8pm

Summit Meadow Cabins　　　503 272-3494
(PO Box 235)
Government Camp OR 97028
Vacation rentals, cabins and homes suitable for 2-12. Two
miles south of Government Camp. Wooded creek-side setting,
miles of trails. Reservations recommended. 9am–9pm, message
phone.

Thunderhead Lodge　　　503 272-3368
87577 Govt. Camp Loop (PO Box 129)
Government Camp OR 97028
Overnight condominium rentals. Studios, 1 bedroom, or 3 bedroom condos with full-size kitchens. Heated swimming pool,
recreation room, ski wax room and storage area for skis/bikes.

Timberline Ski Area & Lodge　　　503 272-3311
Timberline OR 97028
Ski area, hotel, gift shop and food service. A National Historic
Landmark, Timberline Lodge has 70 guest rooms and award-
winning cuisine. Winter and summer skiing. Reservations for
lodging: 800 547-1406.

Trillium Lake Basin Cabins　　　503 272-0151
(PO Box 28)
Government Camp OR 97028
Beautiful new cabins on Mineral Creek, adjacent to Multorpor
Mtn. Explore historic Old Oregon Trail, mountain bike,or sit by
the fire.

Trollhaugen Lodging　　　503 272-3223
30498 E. W'yEast (PO Box 1)
Government Camp OR 97028
2-bedroom units with bath, kitchen, living room, electric heat
and woodburning stove. Firewood, laundry and waxroom
available. In downtown Government Camp.

Zig Zag Inn　　　503 622-4779
70162 E Hwy 26 (PO Box 336, Welches, OR 97067)
Zigzag OR 97049
Casual restaurant in historic log building. Pizza, pasta, burgers,
steak, chicken, vegetarian dishes, old-fashion milkshakes.
Lounge, 3 fireplaces, air conditioned. 4pm–10pm Mon–Fri,
11am–10:30pm Sat, 11am–9pm Sun.

OTHER SERVICES

Alpine Towing 503 622-3365
(PO Box 120)
Rhododendron OR 97049
24-hour towing

The Art of Adventure Raft Trips 503 272-0120
(PO Box 250)
Government Camp OR 97067

C.J.'s Chevron Food Mart 503 622-3017
93770 E. Hwy. 26 (PO Box 2)
Government Camp OR 97028
Ice, Hot deli, espresso, big selection of camping and fishing
supplies, fishing license, boat passes, Warm Springs fishing
permits, tire chains, snow park permits. Summer: 7am–8pm
Mon.-Thurs, 7am-9pm Fri.–Sun.

Mt. Hood Brewing Co. 503 272-0102
87304 E Govt. Camp Loop (PO Box 56)
Government Camp OR 97028
Inquire about tours at the Brew Pub adjacent to the brewery.
Group tours may call ahead.

Mt. Hood Coffee Roasters and Mercantile 503 622-5153
64235 E. Brightwood Loop Rd.
Brightwood OR 97011
Fresh roasting high grade coffee beans on site, fresh roasted
hazelnuts, espresso drinks and sodas, Dolce Syrups, coffee-
related merchandise, local artists' displays. Summer:
10am-6pm Wed.-Sun.

Mt. Hood Ski Bowl Winter & Summer Resort 503 272-3206
(PO Box 280)
Ski Bowl OR 97028

Purdy's Towing 503 622-3153
64025 E. Brightwood Loop Rd. (64025 E. Brightwood Loop Rd.)
Brightwood OR 97011
Lockout, jump start, gas and towing. 24-hour service

Summit Chevron 503 272-3692
90149 E. Government Camp Loop (PO Box 2)
Government Camp OR 97028
Hot deli, espresso, tire chains, snow park permits, beer, wine,
pop, ice, worms, camping and fishing supplies. 7am-8pm daily

The Van Bevers Gallery at Mt. Hood 503 622-5904
24403 E. Welches Rd. (PO Box 891)
Welches OR 97067
Working studio/gallery of Susan VanBevers includes over 25
local artists and craftsmen. Great price range. Museum-quality
gifts and permanent Christmas corner.

*This resource list was extracted from information provided
by the businesses.*

INDEX TO HIKES

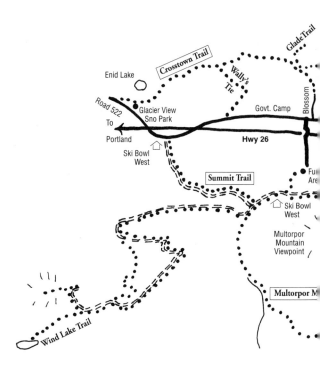

N

Enid Lake

Crosstown Trail

Wally's
Tie

Glade Trail

Road 522

Glacier View
Sno Park

Govt. Camp

Blossom

To
Portland

Hwy 26

Ski Bowl
West

Summit Trail

Fu
Are

Ski Bowl
West

Multorpor
Mountain
Viewpoint

Multorpor M

Wind Lake Trail

0   ½   1
SCALE OF MILES

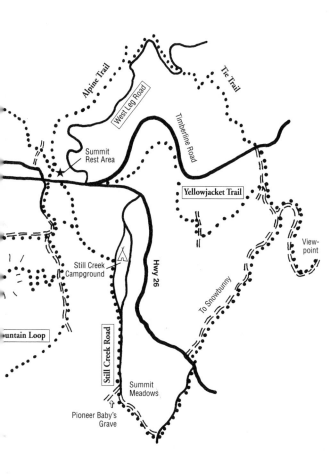